Making Work *Work* for You

Advance Praise

Witty, wise, accessible, and refreshingly female-voiced, Jo McRell's book is a work of au current relevance - like a super savvy BFF sitting with you on the sofa, sipping wine, and sharing invaluable insider secrets of success. Her pithy TLDR key points for each chapter, her real stories and concrete examples, and her humility combined with confidence and experience make for a relatable (and actionable!) read.

—S. Lucia Kanter St. Amour, VP Emerita UN Women, attorney, and author of For the Forces of Good: The Superpower of Everyday Negotiation

I find myself bringing up this book in so many conversations. It's a great source for all the trends in employee experience today. I wish I'd had a guide like this at the start of my career. This book will give people, especially those underrepresented in their workplaces, the confidence that makes all the difference.

—Michele McGovern, editor at HR Morning

We all need to put some new tools in our toolbox as the workplace evolves. Jo has done a great job of creating a guide that will help you balance it all – integrating new tools like AI, developing your business IQ, getting transparent about money at work, and setting personal goals that create more value for you and lead to career success.

—Liz Wilke, economist and future of work researcher, host of The Gustonomics Podcast

This book provides true insider knowledge and a whole new way to frame your career so you can do your most meaningful and valuable work. You'll want to keep this in your back pocket to refer to time and time again.

—Logan Rizzo, communications expert

So many people operate in a world of work that was originally designed for white men - and so many people struggle in that environment. But that doesn't have to be the final word. With this book, you'll see that you have so many more choices and get guidance on how to make the best ones for you. Jo's book is practical, easy to read, and full of new & useful tips for today's workplace. There's so much here that I wish more people knew.

—Paulina Houston, attorney investigator & employment law expert at the Law Office of Paulina Houston

Warm, generous, approachable, and fun - pretty much every coaching client I've worked with would benefit from this book! Jo covers so many sticky topics: job interview homework assignments, compensation top-to-bottom, career-limiting moves, bias, what's up with middle managers, why 'winning from the middle' is a good thing...and so much more.

—Carole-Ann Penney, career strategist & leadership development trainer, Penney Leadership

MAKING WORK WORK FOR YOU

The truth, tips and tools you need to navigate today's workplace and get more of what you want.

Jo McRell

FREE
PERSONAL
CAREER MAP
INCLUDED

Copyright © 2024 Jo McRell
All rights reserved.

Thank you for purchasing an authorized edition of this book and complying with copyright law!

No part of this publication may be used or reproduced in any manner whatsoever without prior written permission of the author, except in the case of brief quotations embodied in reviews and certain other non-commercial uses permitted by copyright law.

Future HER Press
3964 Rivermark Plaza
Unit #2606
Santa Clara, CA 95054

ISBN: 979-8-9906919-0-2 (ebook)
ISBN: 979-8-9906919-1-9 (Paperback)

Book cover image by Mehmooda Sultana.
Formatting by Nadene Seiters.

Disclaimer & Important Information

This book is designed to provide authoritative information on the subject matter covered. The author makes no guarantees for any individual's career as a result of reading this book. All careers are unique, involve risk and depend on the work, skills, timing and environment that come together. This book is sold with the understanding that the publisher is not engaged in rendering legal, accounting, or other professional services. If you require legal or other professional services, you should seek out a competent professional in that field.

Stories, examples and names used in the book represent multiple similar experiences and so have been altered or fictionalized, thus references to any person, living or dead, are not implied.

While the author has made every attempt to provide accurate information at the time of publication, neither the publisher nor the author assumes any responsibility for errors or changes that occur after publication. Furthermore, the author doesn't have control over or assume responsibility for any third-party authors or content owners and their content or websites.

DOWNLOAD YOUR FREE PERSONAL CAREER MAP!

READ THIS FIRST

To say thank you AND make sure you get the absolute most from this book, I would like to give you a personal career map 100% FREE!

This lightweight but powerful workbook will be your personal guide to navigating work and your own career success! Get more out of relationships with your manager, mentors, or career coaching sessions (hopefully this is a development perk your organization offers—if not, ask!). This personalized career map sets you up to:

- know your worth (and negotiate for it!)
- create more value (for yourself and others)
- avoid mistakes (so you can get more of what you want, less of what you don't need)
- build for your future (in this fast changing world of work)

To download go to:

www.jomcrell.com/free

CREATE AMAZING EMPLOYEE EXPERIENCES

Inspired by what you're reading? Have a role influencing the employee experience at your organization?

My company—Jo McRell Consulting—works with organizations of different sizes to improve their employee experience in the #futureofwork. Contact me about:

- Speaking opportunities
- Publication contributions
- Internal communication strategy
- HR program & operations support
- Culture & communications audit
- Leader coaching
- Crisis communications
- Employer brand strategy

To learn more and contact me go to:

www.jomcrell.com

FOLLOW ME FOR MORE INSIGHTS & TIPS

Continue to learn and be inspired! Follow me on LinkedIn and Instagram to get more tips, tools, and truth. You'll see updates on the hottest HR trends from my network—and sometimes we just post for fun!

LinkedIn: www.linkedin.com/in/jomcrell

Instagram: www.instagram.com/jmcrell

Dedication

The most important thing anyone can do is to *give* their best. Otherwise, a world focused on the take becomes an empty one fast. This book is my small gift to pay it forward . . . and pay it back to all those who supported me—especially the women.

There's a special place in heaven for women who support each other.

Table of Contents

Table of Contents

Preface

Hello! I'm Jo

I was frozen. Literally. Three months after moving to Japan, I found out I had a curious condition called Raynaud's which made me susceptible to frostbite. This condition may have been discovered in Paris, but it was definitely not a luxury brand experience. That December in Japan averaged 43°F, and because it was too expensive to have central heating there (in houses, schools, or many office buildings), I just couldn't get warm. By mid-December, I couldn't move most of my fingers and was at risk of losing circulation altogether.

I also couldn't imagine dealing with doctors in a totally different medical system and language. I was a cash-strapped student on scholarships. I couldn't afford the expensive and experimental treatments they prescribed—blood thinners (also used in rat poison!), nerve destroying surgery called sympathectomy, and more no-thank-you options. And I didn't want the hassle for my host family (who were very kind but clearly bewildered and recommended I practically live in an ofuro or bath). So I chose an unconventional solution. I booked the cheapest ticket I could find to the warmest place. Thailand, in this case. I thawed out there nicely while backpacking from Bangkok to Singapore.

Challenges are everywhere. Not everything is in our control. And lots of people will give you advice or push you into “the right way” of doing things. It’s important to know what your full range of options are (or at least as many as you can get access to). But you don’t have to follow the mainstream, the conventional, the recommended or normal way of doing things. You can make your own choices.

Unfortunately, it took a while for me to apply this kind of thinking to my work. I’ll give you one of my you’re-kidding-me examples. It’s about being ghosted:

I had just learned from an inside friend why a recruiter and hiring manager suddenly stopped talking to me after four successful interview rounds. I went through all the emotions: disbelief, anger, sadness, repeat anger (because, come on!), then finally . . . ugh.

Picture this: I’d been interviewing to build a new team with a growing startup. It was the fourth interview round and all smooth sailing. The room was buzzing with positive energy, and I was told I was one of their top two candidates for the final round.

Then, the hiring manager threw out this casual curveball: “*What do you do in your free time?*” Cue my “mistake.” I proudly launched into a story about my amazing stepson’s acapella group (think mini-Glee!) and how he’s composing his own music. We were geeking out over his musical talent.

Later my inside source on the panel (turns out they didn’t know about our connection!) told me what happened. As soon as I walked out of the interview, the hiring manager said: “*Well, we’re not hiring her. It’d be like working with my mom or aunt. Gross!*”

Seriously!?! That wasn't the first or last time I had doors closed to me because I was a working mom—especially in the bro culture of Silicon Valley. But let me tell you, it was a real eye opener about some of the realities of the workplace. You see, early on in my career I was clueless—or more likely I was overly idealistic. I wasn't getting the whole unwritten rules thing—or more likely I was fighting it . . . and it cost me.

The challenge wasn't always about feeling locked out and stuck. Later, I had the opposite problem. I was leading my function for a top brand name, earning great pay, doing all the things. But? I was burnt. Out. Like a crisp. No time for myself. Constant hustle. Saying no felt impossible—everything seemed crucial for success. I'd mastered some of the workplace rules (like keeping my personal life, well . . . personal), but I was still stuck.

Looking back on my career, I can see the rollercoaster ride it was. Working with industry giants, leading teams through major transitions, traveling the world, and helping shape a new era of work have been incredible highs. There have been lows too—layoffs, soul-crushing bosses, petty politics, the constant struggle to balance work and family, the burden of taking on too much.

Piled on to that were all the people I met feeling their own version of stuck. For all kinds of reasons—race, neurodiversity, gendered expectations, socioeconomic background, fill in the blank—so many people were hitting brick walls in their own work lives.

I want to share what I learned: Challenges are inevitable. The key is to choose them wisely, to make them count. **The difference between empowerment and simply reacting to circumstance lies in understanding your choices.** Taking on a challenge as a choice is a completely different experience than facing one because you have no other option.

The landscape of work is changing rapidly, and the challenges we face will require new strategies and fresh perspectives. **This book is my attempt to empower you to make conscious and better choices in your career.** We'll explore the twists and turns of the modern workplace. We'll explore ways to develop your skillsets, navigate complex situations, and advocate for yourself. With each challenge you choose to take on, you'll understand your priorities better, build confidence, and open doors to new opportunities.

So join me on this journey—let's rewrite the rules, embrace flexibility, and create a career that lets us truly shine. We'll do it all with the understanding that **empowerment comes from setting yourself up to have more choices.** Get ready to make work *work* for you.

Introduction

TLDR - Work, well . . . takes work. But it shouldn't drain the life out of you. In fact, work should be one of the ways you get more of what you want—living your passions, making some money, finding opportunities, and creating great connections. Getting there has always been more difficult for those less privileged in the workplace (like women and people of color). Add to that significant changes to flexibility, AI and upskilling, and the options for success. That makes now the time to understand how to navigate this blend of the old and the new, the challenges and the opportunities.

By the end of this book, you'll have the tools, tips, and the truth about today's workplaces needed to make work *work* for you. Along the way we'll uncover some stories and insights to make sure that you: know your worth, create more value for yourself and others, avoid career-limiting problems, and build for your future. Get ready to love your work (or at least, love what it gets you!).

You're likely to spend about 1,850 hours working this year. Over your lifetime, that's over 90,000 hours total. It's a third of your life.[i] Does that number make you want to cry? It does me, a little . . . actually, a lot. The only thing you'll spend more time doing (possibly) is sleeping. So you want all these hours to mean something, right? To be interesting. To connect you to great people. To learn new things. To make you feel proud of what you can accomplish. To be fun (at least occasionally). To make you feel fulfilled. To help you realize your passions. To bring enough money into your life so you can enjoy the other two-thirds.

I want all of these things for you too. And more than that, I want you to have choices—choices about where you work, how you work, how much you work, and with whom. That's what this book is about.

You will no longer feel the weight of office politics and drama. You'll no longer wonder why you seem to be speaking a different language than your manager. You'll no longer fear being automated out of a job. You'll no longer think work-life balance is a joke. You'll no longer worry that only the bros have power in the workplace. You'll no longer get stuck with a low-ball salary or performance rating. Instead, you'll know your value, get paid for it, and use that value to get more of what you want in your career—all while having better relationships with the people around you.

I also want you to be prepared for the changing world of work (think: remote and hybrid, artificial intelligence [AI], up to five generations in one increasingly diverse workplace, fractional work and side hustles, the transition to the Sharing or Creative Economies, and more). I want the work that you do today to lead to a more fulfilling life, a better use of your time, and better-paid work. I want your work to be something you look forward to, instead of feeling the dread of the Sunday Scaries.

The good news is that you can have this. This book will give you the truth about work, the tools and the pro tips to make work *work* for you. And, along the way, we're going to banish some painful myths, get the real story on how organizations operate, laugh a little, better understand ourselves so we can be our own best champions, and maybe cut a few onions. It'll be cathartic . . . and not too much work, I promise.

Together, we're going to tackle and get rid of the obstacles in your path. We're going to get a grip on this changing world of work post-pandemic. We're going to understand the difference between your dream job and a perfect job (BTW, you want the dream job). We're going to weigh the tradeoffs in the workplace and get you more of what you want, less of what you don't need. We're going to understand the most common problems in the workplace so you know how to avoid or fix them. By the end of this book, you're going to have a personalized career map and all the tools you need to navigate your way to work that fuels your life.

Who This Book Is For

This book is for the women who are sweating it out, trying to grow in the glass greenhouses of so many workplaces. This book is for people of color feeling lonely and underserved by the structures and groups around them. This book is for those who don't "fit" with automatic ease in the one-size-fits-all environments around them. This book is for people who didn't come from well-to-do corporate backgrounds full of role models for success and the "right" connections. This book is for people feeling stuck and needing to hit the big red reset button on their work life. This book is for Millennials and GenZers who don't see their success tied to any one particular company and instead are wondering how to pursue multiple passions and own their career and time.

If you're a knowledge-based worker, a professional—a.k.a. paid to think—if you're employed by an organization who sets the rules of work, and if you're trying to navigate the early to middle part of your career, then this book is for you.

Disclaimer Alert #1: When I say "work," "job," or "career," that could mean a variety of things to you. Lots of people today are mixing full-time work with side hustles or freelancing or balancing their time between part-time gigs or working on a passion project along with their day job (a.k.a. fractional work). To keep it simple, in this book I'm talking about how to get more out of any work you do for an organization as an employee and a professional (regardless of what your work mix looks like). At times I'm using "job" in the singular because the focus is on how to get more out of each work opportunity. More than half of workers in America are doing just this—working as a professional in some capacity—and if you're reading this book, then I assume you are too.

Disclaimer Alert #2: The world of work is undergoing massive change—finally. The old model from the Post World War II era—the 9-5 commute to the office largely focused on (white) men supporting single-income traditional families that was epitomized in the TV series *Mad Men*—is finally being revolutionized. While the pandemic accelerated this revolution, it hasn't all shaken out yet.

Employers are struggling with a number of changes:

- Flexibility and more distributed work with remote and hybrid
- Increasingly diverse and multigenerational workforces
- Generative artificial intelligence (Gen AI) and its impact on automating work
- Business challenges like changes in how readily money is flowing in capital markets
- Workers voting with their feet by taking on fractional work—like the gig economy and entrepreneurship
- Skill gaps leading to an increased focus on skills vs. pedigrees (like college degrees and MBA credentials)

We, as individual workers, are moving through this change curve faster than most organizations that have large-scale processes and investments in old ways of running a business. That means we will own more of our own career development and success in the future. I see so much opportunity in these changes. But there will also be plenty of challenges in navigating the often turbulent waters of change in the meantime. I want you to have as much insight and as many resources as you can to make great choices for you as we push through the messy birth of this "future of work."

Disclaimer Alert #3: This book is definitely not the only one written for working professionals. In fact, there are countless books, articles, podcasts, vlogs, and so much more on the world of work. But most of these resources are specifically for executive leaders or startup entrepreneur founders (about 12x the number of these types of books exist vs. books written for the average professional). No offense—great for those leaders—but they've already got a number of resources supporting them. What about you? I believe you deserve the best knowledge and resources you can get.

Not only that but the majority of books for professionals on the market were written pre-pandemic—without the current context of the changing world of work. Many existing resources are also hyper-focused on one particular dynamic of work. For example: getting your first job, getting promoted, how to present in the workplace, etc. There are a lot of great resources out there; I'll reference several of my faves. But there are very few books that help you navigate the workplace of today. Even fewer focus on women, people of color, and people who find that the "culture fit" of many workplaces doesn't fit them. And none will give you a personalized career map to navigate the changing world of work. This book is all that. It's written for you—and it's written to empower you in the future of work.

Disclaimer Alert #4: I've included a lot of real-life example stories throughout the book. To keep it simple, I share these stories through the eyes of a particular person. But I picked these stories to share because they represent a common experience I've seen many times across the span of my career, network, and research. In each story I give this person a name, but it's a name I made up to represent all the people who've experienced that situation. Again, I'm focused on the experiences of women and underrepresented workers. That's why you'll also see I use the pronouns "she" and "they."

Why I Wrote This Book

Before I wrote this book, I spent over 15 years on the inside. Across multiple types of organizations—from nonprofits to startups to global giants with 100K+ employees—my roles in internal communication and employee experience were at the center of everything that was happening. I've been an individual contributor, people manager, and executive leader. I've worked as a close partner to every type of C-suite leader and organization (CEO, COO, CPO, CRO, CTO, CCO, and more Cs). Some of the leaders I've worked with were inspiring and amazing human beings (thank you!) . . . some not so much. Either way, I've learned from all of them. I've worked within marketing, as part of specific product business units, within strategy and operations, the office of the CEO, and most frequently under HR (Human Resources or the People organization). I've been through intense hiring periods (doubling the number of employees in one year), as well as layoffs at multiple companies (once I even had to lay myself off). I've sat behind closed doors with the executive team, seeing first-hand how decisions about changing models of work are considered and made. Now I'm making my living using my experience, expertise, and passion to work for myself as a solopreneur. Work is changing, and I'm happy to be changing with it.

I've also lived and worked in a number of countries and places around the world. I've adapted to a variety of different lifestyles and cultural norms—in Japan, Mexico, Switzerland, the Midwest, the Southwest, the West—you get the idea. In fact, that's a big part of what motivates me. Learning from others, being surprised, looking at how we live and make choices in our various realities. This all fascinates me. I've mentored (formally and informally) hundreds of people over my career, and I usually learn as much from them as they do me. That's one reason I took the leap at this point to be a solopreneur. I wanted to dive into the deep end of this new era of work and explore what these changes might mean for workers—both opportunities and challenges. I wanted to talk to and learn from a wide variety of people across the workplace experience. It's sort of a gestalt thing—the sum of all those conversations and experiences really do create something bigger. This book is a chance to share that collective wisdom and lived experience with you.

Across all of these different experiences, I've seen the good, bad, and the ugly. I've had an unvarnished view of how organizations make decisions and view their employees AND how employee perspectives about employers are changing. I've seen hundreds of employee cases come through HR, and the many different mistakes many employees (often unknowingly) make. I've seen employment trends shift multiple times and how career trajectories change with them. I've had the honor of working directly in diversity, equity, inclusion, and belonging (DEIB) and learning from the perspectives of coworkers from underrepresented communities. (NOTE: I'm a straight, white, cisgender woman. I definitely can't speak for everyone. Instead, I've consciously sought to make my work, including this book, inclusive of underrepresented or disadvantaged experiences.)

Throughout my career I've worked hard, I was smart, and I knew how to get leaders to trust me. So it all went perfectly. Right? NO. I've made a LOT of mistakes myself. I've banged my head on the proverbial brick wall. Hated my boss and as a result lost my job. Said the stupid thing in front of way too many people. Landed myself in dead-end roles. Been bored. Been overworked (I once worked 90 hours/week for almost half a year. NOT recommended.) And I've made many other mistakes I can't even remember. But my biggest mistake was spending too many years and roles early in my career blissfully ignorant of what I was doing with myself. Instead I sort of just expected it would happen. Notice the "it" here? What the hell is "it" anyway? I learned the hard way that if you don't know your priorities, someone else will decide them for you. That landed me in a place I didn't want to be—a place I took a while to climb out of.

I've seen hundreds of my coworkers frustrated, stuck, and stressed over the years. Being stressed at work is apparently a very common American experience—increasingly so. Something like 80% of workers say their job stresses them out and over 50% say they need help to fix it.[ii] Post-pandemic this seems to be getting worse, with around 84% of people saying mental, physical, and financial health is now their top priority to improve.[iii] Meanwhile, employee engagement is going down, the lowest it's been in years,[iv] which shows that people aren't getting their top priorities met in the workplace. It's not surprising then that company loyalty is also at an all-time low.[v] Feeling any of this?

Empowering You with Choice

You are not alone! And with the right tools, tips, and insider truths, I want you to get to the model of work you love—avoiding burnout and problems while getting more of what you want. Now that the world of work has finally been catapulted into the future by the pandemic (wobbly—yes! But evolving), I want you to have the best map possible to navigate this new era of work—and all its possibilities and challenges.

Over my career experiences, through the eyes of others, and in my research, I've seen over and over that the most powerful thing you can have is choices. Once I realized what my choices were, how to create more choices, and how to match my goals with the choices around me, I got more of what I wanted out of work and had a lot of career successes on my terms. With more resources, knowledge about your own goals, and the truth about how workplaces really operate and how they're changing today, you can also have more choices in your career path. Ultimately, that's what this book is about—empowering you with choice.

How to Read This Book

So how can you use this book to make sure your work fuels your life?

In the pages of *Making Work* Work *for You,* I'll give you a personalized career map to navigate the future of work. I've uncovered the tools, tips, and truths you need to make work *work* for you. You'll not only be able to make your current job(s) much more worthwhile but take the next steps to create a career that fuels your life.

Section one is all about knowing your worth, where you'll:

- Chapter 1: Get The Full Picture Of Rewards (Both Monetary And Non-Monetary)
- Chapter 2: Negotiate Salary and Beyond
- Chapter 3: Get Rich Sooner Than Later

In Section two you'll learn more about creating more value (for yourself and others):

- Chapter 4: Under-Promise and Over-Deliver
- Chapter 5: Get Specific About What's Valuable to You
- Chapter 6: See The Value In Others (And They Will Help Put Your Career On A Rocket Ship to Success)

Section three tackles how to avoid common problems (or as HR calls them "career-limiting moves"):

- Chapter 7: Avoid Hating Your Manager
- Chapter 8: Avoid Career-Limiting Moves
- Chapter 9: Avoid A Bad Performance Review
- Chapter 10: Avoid A Bad Exit

Section four focuses specifically on helping you build for your future (in the future of work):

- Chapter 11: Flexibility and Autonomy
- Chapter 12: AI and Upskilling
- Chapter 13: The Productivity Crisis

Don't feel you have to read this book exactly as it was laid out. Skip to chapters that feel most relevant. Use the TLDRs at the beginning of each chapter to ground yourself in the key takeaways. Find pro tips in the bang boxes. Check out the resources and references included. However you get there, by the closing of this book, you'll have developed your own personal career map with all the tools, tips, and truth about workplaces you need.

I won't assume you're like everyone else reading this book. Your own journey is unique. Have your priorities straight and are ready to set specific, actionable goals to get you to the next step? Go straight to chapter 5. Want to get a better sense of the changing work landscape before diving into your own personal career map? Dive into section four. Feeling like you need to hit reset on your career, but not sure if you're swimming in "career-limiting move" quicksand? Head over to section three. Hating your boss and trying to decide if you should jump ship or fix the relationship? Then chapter 7 is for you.

Wherever you start and end, this book will give you the tools, tips, and truths you need to create your own personal career map. This isn't like a pirate's treasure map where you have to steal from others and only get the treasure at the end of a long, arduous, dangerous journey wearing salty and sweat-encrusted frilly shirts. Ugh. This is more like *Super Mario Brothers* with treasure all along the way, lots of friends to help you win the superpowers you need to get to the next level, and super-cute outfits. I'll help you design your own personalized career map at each step. Get ready to take action. Your career is yours to love!

Section One

Know Your Worth

TLDR—Knowing your worth is a superpower. It's one you need to create a meaningful career. It's not just about a paycheck—your skills, experience, and potential all add up. In this section we'll talk about how to do your research so you know what's possible (financially and otherwise!). Since you'll make tradeoffs throughout your career, we'll get you set up to nail your priorities, win your financial freedom, and have more (and better!) choices.

If I ask you *what's your worth*, are you thinking about annual salary or savings in the bank? That's how most people would answer this question. Well, I think you're worth much more than a number. You should too. So let's try again. What's your worth?

I'd argue that your worth is the sum total of many different things. Sure, money in hand is a part of it, but so are your experiences, unique talents, ability to learn, earning potential, the point of view only you can bring based on your background, relationship skills and network, personality, and so much more. The more you understand your total worth and how to showcase it, the more others around you will see your worth.

Let's take a page out of Whitney Houston's book. The story goes that lawyer and music industry agent Clive Davis first noticed her singing "Greatest Love of All" at her mother's regular club gig. Clive was so inspired he offered Whitney her first record deal practically on the spot. I feel pretty inspired by that song too. Whitney's voice was beyond amazing, but those lyrics are pretty great as well. They tell us that YOU are the greatest love of all. You've got to know yourself. You've got to be proud of yourself. You've got to believe in yourself to succeed. This song is all about knowing your own worth—and not letting someone else decide it for you. It doesn't just make for an epic song; it's great advice for life and work.

So don't take your worth—and all the different aspects that make you unique—for granted. In this section I'll walk you through the full picture of key things to consider (monetary and nonmonetary) that recognize and reflect your worth in the workplace and then give you an easy exercise to kick off your personal career map by writing down how you want to define your worth. This is the foundation you need to make work *work* for you. Let's dig in and break it down.

Chapter 1

Get the Full Picture

TLDR—Stuck on a base salary number? Let's get unstuck. There are a whole range of benefits that come with different work environments (both money and beyond the money). Do you crave a top salary and fast-paced environment? Or is a zen work culture and strong mentorship more your vibe? Understanding what those options are and what truly matters to *you* is the key. Do that, and you'll get more of what you want, less of what you don't need.

Monetary Benefits

Let's start with monetary benefits—a.k.a. the money. Unless you're a lucky trust-fund baby, won the lottery (and still have something after taxes), or something else equally lovely, we all need money. Me included. Now I'll be the first to advocate that work is definitely *not* all about the money . . . but we'll get to that, don't you worry.

So back to the money. . . . When most people think about how much a job pays, they only think about base salary. Most companies only advertise that number with the job description as well. But that's not the full picture. Introducing **total rewards.** Total rewards (or the total value of how a company invests in you) can include lots of great payouts. NOTE: Many of these rewards are only offered to full-time employees—a consideration when thinking about your needs and your work mix. I strongly encourage you to learn about these various rewards so you understand what's possible and so you can negotiate (see chapter 2) for what you need and get the most out of your rewards package:

- **Base pay**—This is your basic salary number. It's the fixed amount your employer agreed to pay for your time and services per your role. This could be an hourly rate, monthly income, or annual salary.
- **Benefits**—These usually include: medical, dental, and vision insurance plans; time off and leave policies; and can also include mental health resources, career coaching sessions, wellness programs, educational funds or programs, etc.
- **Pay increases**—This is typically an annual increase to your base salary and can be based on either merit (your performance) or may be a cost-of-living adjustment to help your salary stay in line with the price of regular household expenses.
- **Bonus**—This is above and beyond base pay that is usually performance-based (for company and/or individual performance) and can be paid out in cash or equity. Bonus programs can be annual, biannual, and/or spot (awarded in the moment for a specific accomplishment).
- **Commission**—This is money paid for reaching specific goals, usually selling a certain amount of goods or services. Commission can be paid on top or instead of a regular base salary.

- **Match funds**—These funds apply toward savings you make in a company-sponsored program, the most typical being 401K retirement or student loan payback. Another possible type of match fund could be a health-savings account (HSA)—set up with a high deductible medical coverage plan, if that's the right plan for you.
    - If you set aside money from your paycheck (pre-taxes) to go into these funds, some companies will match your savings up to a certain percentage—a.k.a. free money, not taxed, not performance-based.
- **Perks**—Many companies offer a unique set of discounts, funds, or rewards programs based on what's important to the company culture and employee needs. Examples include: food and bev services in-office (definitely need that coffee after the commute!), work anniversary awards, commuting or home office funds, wellness funds, pet insurance, caregiver support and funds, community or social cause funds / donation match / volunteer support, sponsoring sports leagues, office and tech supplies, coworking space membership, travel and expenses coverage, etc.
    - NOTE: Some perks are time bound—example: when starting a new position starting bonus, relocation funds, temporary company housing or similar might be possible.
- **Equity**—This is payment in the form of part ownership in the company you work for. Like getting little slices of the company pie. Equity can include: restricted stock units (RSUs), employee stock purchase programs (ESPP), options, etc.
    - Equity award grants are generally valued between 10-50% of your base salary (depending on the industry,

your level or seniority, how competitive the talent market is, etc.).
    - The better the company performs (high growth, high profits), the more your equity is worth.
    - The point of equity is not immediate gratification. It's to help employers reward you for sticking around multiple years (longer tenure).
    - In fact, many equity award grants have a one-year cliff—meaning you can't collect unless you've stayed with the company for at least 12 months.
    - If you are granted shares or stock (RSUs) as part of your total rewards package, that stock award (or your piece of the pie) will usually be granted in small slices each quarter over a three- to four-year period until you get your full piece.
    - You can't access this equity until after it vests (vesting = the date the stock transfers to your ownership), and you can't cash out (or liquidate) that equity unless the company is public (or your private company sets up a liquidation event–often called a tender offer).

Here's an example of what a total rewards package could look like:

Let's assume a $100,000 base salary with typical benefits coverage. We'll add in a typical 3% annual merit increase to your base salary and a moderate equity grant (at 30% of annual base salary) that will take four years to vest. *(Note: this example does not include perks.)*

- Base Salary: $100,000
- Benefits: $10,000

    - Medical Plan: $6,000
    - Other Benefits: $4,000 (like 401K or student-loan match)
- RSUs (Year 1 Value): $30,000
- Total Rewards (at the end of Year 1): $140,000

Let's say that you stay for four years (the full vesting cycle for your equity grant). We'll add in a typical 3% annual merit increase and give you a typical 7% bonus at year two. Because you're a high performer (hell yes!), we'll assume a promotion at year three with a raise of 11% and an additional equity award grant of $50,000 (four-year vesting). What would your total rewards be at the end of four years?

- Base Salary: $435,089.90
- Year 2 Bonus: $7,210
- Year 3 Promotion Raise: $17,229.02 (11% raise applied to the base salary from year three onward)
- Year 3 Promotion Equity Grant: $50,000 (with $12,500 vested by end of year four)
- Benefits: $40,000
- RSUs (Original + Additional Equity): $132,500 ($120,000 original + $12,500 from the additional equity grant)
- Total Rewards: $614,799.90

Wow! Good stuff, right? Almost $615,000 after four years is NOT the same as just thinking about $400,000 of base salary. Yet many people don't ask about the total rewards package when negotiating a new job or comparing job offers. And unfortunately, many employees don't use the total rewards available to them after they join. For example, 47% of employees at a previous company where I worked missed out on hundreds of dollars each year just in the perks category, and a recent survey showed more than half of workers don't understand their benefits[vi]—ouch! I know people (super-smart, high-IQ people) who never used their company perks because they didn't know where to find the perks page on the intranet. Lots of people I've worked with didn't know that most medical insurance plans cover mental health services—and suffered needlessly.

It can be a little complicated! Confused about 401K plans, equity awards, or commission-based pay? No worries. Do a search for equity compensation, and you're on your way. There are lots of great videos and resources out there. Nerd Wallet, Indeed, investment firms like Fidelity, and online learning platforms will all have info for you.

Regardless, please do your homework. Ask your manager or HR. Get to know all the rewards your company offers, and use everything meaningful to you. I hate throwing money away. How about you?

Pro Tip for Fractional Workers

If you're a gig worker or are thinking about quitting a full-time job with benefits to turn your side hustle into your primary thing, I applaud you. Love your energy and focus on what makes you happy. BUT if you end up with no healthcare coverage or no retirement savings, you'll quickly lose control over finances, which greatly limits your work decisions . . . and that could make you very unhappy.

I highly recommend collecting a paycheck with benefits—especially health care and 401k or student-loan payback and retirement benefits—during at least the first ten years of your career. If you do think you have enough financial freedom to live the fully fractional life, make sure you have enough savings for at least six months and that you're still able to put some savings away to invest each year.

Counting on a partner to bring in the benefits bacon? Cool. But keep your own retirement or investment accounts going. I hope your relationship is a long-term success. Still this is America, and with a 50% divorce rate and an average relationship length of two years, you should always put your own oxygen mask on first.

OK, so now that you know what could be available, how do you prioritize what to look for? Depending on what you have going on in your life—digging out of school loan debt, saving up for that Taylor Swift concert ticket, coming back from a gap year, looking for mental health support, buying a house, raising kids, dealing with a health issue, nervous about retirement, etc.—how you negotiate and use the total rewards package matters. It might even change the type of organization you want to work for.

Case in Point: I've worked at multiple companies oriented toward two different employee types. Not surprisingly the reward packages were very different. I've got a couple of examples below. Here, one worked well for my life needs . . . and the other actually became a drain on my life.

Company 1—Let's call it "Perky Perks." The rewards package at Perky Perks was targeted to early career, single professionals. Their perks game was full-on and famous: on-campus services like free dry cleaning; numerous cafes with food from around the world to serve you breakfast, lunch, and dinner; gym facilities with personal trainers, massage chairs, swimming pools, and high-end locker rooms; dog parks for your pet; regular Happy Hours; foosball, pool, and video game rooms; and so much more. All of this was designed to keep people at the office working as long as possible. As lovely as this all sounded, it was not great for me. I was raising a kid and needed to commute long hours. My life at that time was very centered on home and family. The pressure to spend extra hours at the office, hanging out and socializing, was time consuming and not helping my family. The pay was great and the perks were worth a lot of money. Sadly, most of those perks were not only a waste for my needs; they were a stressor.

Company 2—Let's call it "Steady Eddy." The rewards programs at Steady Eddy were targeted to mid-career professionals with families or people running a small business on the side. Steady Eddy generally had a 9-5 mentality. Although my base pay definitely wasn't top dollar, they had generous 401K match and ESPP programs. Their perks program was a spot bonus program run through a partner vendor that converted those spot bonus points into dollars that could be applied to trips, household goods, home services, and more. Since I joined Steady Eddy at a time when my partner and I were buying our first house and raising a family, I used my total rewards package to save tons of money and time on things I needed for this lifestyle (family vacations, furniture, gifts for family and friends, home services, etc.). Because I took the time to understand how this perks system worked, in one year alone I earned tens of thousands of dollars' worth of points to use on things that were meaningful for my family. This was on top of my base salary, performance bonus, and other benefits. Score!

Steady Eddy also had a strong and well organized focus on employee development. I used that focus to grow my role scope, experiences (like becoming a people manager for the first time), and moving into new roles that gave me exposure to different parts of the business. This has been super valuable to my long-term career success and motivated me to stay with the company for almost five years. Another benefit from my long tenure with Steady Eddy was a well-funded stock account with both RSU and ESPP vested funds that have only grown in value over time. In fact, over time, that equity became worth more than my total salary over my five years there. If I had job hopped after year two for a base salary bump, I would have missed out on a lot of equity value, and I wouldn't have developed the relationships I needed to earn all those spot bonus points in the perk system.

Your situation and needs may be totally different than mine were at that time when Steady Eddy was such a good bet for my career. What's important is that you have a good handle on what's top value in your life outside of work. Then you can better make decisions and negotiate for the rewards that improve your life and needs. You do you. Or as the Europeans say: *Work to live, don't live to work.*

If you're early in your career and see work as a way to meet more people, fill up your social schedule and get lots of freebies, then go for it. If your experience with mental health means you're not comfortable socializing in an office and get a lot more out of an autonomous work style, home office equipment, or something else, then go for that. You know your own needs best.

And this brings us to the nonmonetary benefits of what work can offer. There's a lot of goodness that doesn't have a dollar sign next to it. Let's look at all the opportunities to get more of what you need beyond what goes into your paycheck.

Nonmonetary Benefits

Now that we've talked money, we can talk about the other half of the equation. This is just as important. Why? Remember, we spend a third of all our time working—eight hours a day, 40 hours a week, plus or minus—all working out to about 90,000 hours in a lifetime. Most of us need something more than money to feel fulfilled during those hours. And besides, your current pay is just that—a temporary number. The average American also changes jobs at least 12 times in their career (Bureau of Labor Statistics)—and that's historical data. In this new era of work, we're not just changing jobs; we're often changing careers multiple times.

Given all this, multiple other factors besides your paycheck will influence your day-to-day satisfaction and what's possible for your next career move. Let's start with a look at the most important nonmonetary factors influencing how dreamy work can be. You can use this info to take a fresh look at how to get more from your current work environment or to help you assess new organizations and opportunities. Later in chapter 3 we'll work on your personal priorities and how to weigh out both the monetary and nonmonetary factors.

So nonmonetary benefits:

Title vs. Levels: Let's get this one out of the way. Titles are a legacy of old, traditional ways of working. Still, I get it. Your title can be a source of pride (or frustration) and often has salary implications tied to it. Generally, titles mean more in the context of bigger, more mature, hierarchical companies or later in your career. Increasingly today, many people make up their own title (especially true on

LinkedIn—are you in on this game? Wink, wink), and titles are beginning to have less meaning for career progress overall.

It's like the mix and mingle at a friend's wedding. You meet someone new and ask, "*So what do you do?*" and they answer, "*I'm the Head of [company name]'s Customer Experience Strategy.*" Hmmm, good for them. I don't know about you, but I'm much more interested in what people actually do, not their meant-to-impress, likely-to-be-somewhat-fake-news title. Moving on.

Titles are kind of like base salary numbers . . . only part of the picture. I recommend you don't overly fixate on them. However, it's always a good idea to do your research and understand what they mean in your industry or field.

I do recommend you understand levels. Levels are the categories of responsibility, experience, and leadership in an organization. A common leveling system has ten levels (L1 = intern or new college graduate up to L10 = senior executive). Most companies tie salary ranges to levels. And instead of levels, some companies call these pay or salary bands (setting a pay range for each level of role type and experience). Knowing what level or band you're being hired into and what that means for development opportunities and salary expectations can be very helpful.

Insider Truth: People generally progress quickly through the first few levels at the early career stage. It's not uncommon to get a promotion every year or two. The middle of the range (like L4-L5) is where things seem to slow down. These levels often have wider ranges of salary and performance expectations. This is when job responsibilities become more self-directed, more abstract, and when some people make the transition to people manager.

Without understanding how levels work, what your current level is and what your manager and company culture assess for at different levels, many people get stuck, frustrated, and make career-limiting moves. Not to worry, we'll talk more about how to avoid common problems in section three.

People and Networking Connections: At work, who you work with matters as much as what you do and how you do it. You want to connect with people around you who are going to add value. Are you a social butterfly and feel like a networking native? Good, let's fine-tune your approach and narrow in on the relationships most valuable to you. Are you an introvert and dread chatting with people you don't know? No problem, networking doesn't mean you have to become a social butterfly. Networking shouldn't just be about meaningless small talk. It's an opportunity to make meaningful connections—to explore shared interests, learn, and add to your own skills and experience.

Either way, I want you to have a clear focus on the types of people an organization will bring you into contact with—people who can help you on your path to creating your dream job (or make your life miserable). You want to think about the impact these people will have not just in a current role but how they may help or hinder you throughout your career. Oprah in her infinite wisdom said, *"Surround yourself only with people who are going to lift you higher."* Let's take a close look at who those people could be:

- **Bosses**—You likely want to have a great relationship with your manager; it is one of the reasons you will take a job. That's all good. But the chances that your manager will change at least once are pretty high. Take a look at online reviews to get a sense of general management or leadership style (e.g., Glassdoor, Indeed, ZipRecruiter, and maybe Blind keeping in mind who generally posts there—the cynics, etc.) We'll talk more about the relationship with your boss in chapter 7.

- **Peers**—Your coworkers are the people you'll spend most of your work time with and often people you'll bump into time and again as you change roles throughout your career. It's a small world after all. While you can't like absolutely everyone (if you can, message me and let me know your secret), you can use online reviews, ask to talk to a peer-level person during your interview process, and look up alumni from an organization on a platform like LinkedIn to see where people go in their career after working at a specific organization to get a general idea of the type of people who will be your peers. Look good? Fantabulous! Not interesting or see red flags? Something to keep in mind.
- **Communities**—Increasingly organizations help employees connect with each other around similar interests and identity experiences (often called employee resource groups or ERGs). This can be a great way to find your inner circle. An organization's career page will often showcase the types of ERGs they have. Ask to talk to or reach out to an ERG lead to get some perspective.
- **Mentors and Sponsors**—Essentially the difference is a mentor coaches you in areas you want to develop and a sponsor champions you by nominating you for better opportunities. Your boss doesn't have to be your end-all-be-all influencer. Are there interesting people working around you who you can learn from? Making them a mentor and developing that relationship into a sponsor is a great way to

go. You can ask about existing mentorship programs or seek out your own mentors.

- **Customers**—Who an organization's customers or clients are will make a big difference in that organization's culture. My corporate tech career was all centered on serving small business owners. That gave me a sense of purpose, exposed me to all types of creative individuals bringing their own passions to life as a business owner, and attracted coworkers who loved to champion others. That was my jam. What's yours?
- **Partners**—Organizations often need to lean on other organizations to fill in gaps in running their business or amplify the value they offer in serving customers. The types of partners an organization works with can expose you to different kinds of projects, industries, and fields and expand your network outside of your immediate organization.
- **Conferences & Training**—This used to be the center of professional networking taking place in convention centers and hotels. It has been an opportunity as well for people to build influence in their field by showing up as presenters. Those are still happening and IRL has its value, but less formal gatherings in person and online around shared interest topics are starting to create more opportunities for different kinds of networking. Try asking people you admire what their top events or trainings are.
- **Social Networks**—Social media has its place and you can find influencers, recruiters, communities, and other useful relationships here. Organizations will attract their own set of social media followers and influencers; this is something you may find useful ways to tap into.
  NOTE: make sure you follow your organization's social

media policy or guidance. There's lots of opportunity here, but you can also get yourself in trouble if done wrong (see more in Chapter 8: Career Limiting Moves).

There's so much opportunity here. Make sure you think about the various "who's who" that will be part of your career success. Looking for advice on how to flex your people skills and get more out of these relationships? I like how you're thinking! We'll definitely talk more about this in section two.

Experiences: Gaining experience on the job is one of the best ways to advance in your career, hone in on what you love and hate doing most, and get exposure to new ideas and people. So the types of experiences you get out of a job should net positive. What do I mean specifically by experiences, you ask? Lots of potential here: building role-specific skills, learning leadership skills—project or people management, gaining business acumen, applying skills in different types of environments—company/market size or stage of growth, etc.

Personal Example: One of my best experiences was at a company that prioritized design thinking. FYI (if you haven't run across it): design thinking is a people-centered approach to solving problems and coming up with innovative solutions. Everyone at the company—from facilities staff to HR to sales to product teams—were encouraged to think of their work as designing and delivering an innovative product. The company invested in resources, training, events, team workshop facilitators, awards and recognition programs, and the like for any employee who wanted to learn. I personally got a lot out of this development investment—not just formal training but applying it in work projects. And many of my peers went on to become senior leaders at well-known brands because of the reputation we gained as innovative thinkers.

Here's a different example: McKinsey ran a research study on employee development and found on-the-job group learning experiences are strongly linked to salary potential. Specifically, companies that offered cohort hiring or academy training for new hires really paid off—both for those people to develop their skills and in making more money.[vii]

Organizations can offer many types of experiences depending on what their focus is. But it's good to find out what types of investments in employees they do make.

Environment: Organizations each have their own unique environments. I don't mean culture more broadly. I've specifically avoided that term as it means sooo many different things to sooo many people. It's an everything-AND-the-kitchen-sink kind of word. Besides, I think I've done a great job of covering the key aspects of culture here. So here under Environment, I'm going to focus on aspects of what drives the business or output of an organization and how that can impact the employee experience in turn.

While not an exhaustive list, here are some things I recommend you consider:

- **Standard Working Hours and Norms**: Does the company work 9-5 or around the clock? Is it global (crossing time zones and cultures), US only, or regional? Does the company have a location-based policy (in office, hybrid, remote)? What level of flexibility is the leadership team comfortable with? (More on flexibility in chapter 11.)
- **Formality**: How much time and cost will working in an organization take to keep up appearances? Does the image the company projects align with your own self-image?

- **Community Commitments:** Does the organization have an environmental, social, and governance (ESG) commitment? Are they committed to improving diversity, equity, inclusion, and belonging (DEIB)—increasingly relabeled as equity, inclusion, and diversity (EID)? Do they have senior leaders of color, multiple genders, etc.? Do they encourage employee participation in community engagement?
- **Business Model**: This is how the organization creates value. It can be driven by different things and therefore emphasize different skill sets and opportunities (some key categories here):
    - **Product**: These organizations are delivering something unique in the market. They are usually driven by the product department and are focused on being first-to-market or pushing out new features. This environment can be great for engineers, product managers, user experience designers, data scientists and analysts, etc.
    - **Marketing**: Here, the organization's product or service may not be so unique. Instead the emphasis is on how it's brought to market, advertised, and sold. This environment can be a great opportunity for honing expertise in marketing, sales, PR, business development, etc.
    - **Operational**: Here, the focus is on the margin (the difference between profits and expenses). It's as much about saving money as making it because the organization is in a crowded market without a unique product, in a high-risk market, or serving customers at scale who don't have the ability to pay premiums. This can be a great opportunity for finance, analysts,

strategy and operations, former consultants, project managers, etc.

  - **Service**: This type of organization is offering assistance, resources, or skills. You can include a wide range of organizations here: hair salons, construction, education, consulting, real estate, and more. People skills plus a unique skill set are often super, super key for roles in this type of work.

- **Business Stage**: Building a company involves growing through distinct stages; each has its own challenges and opportunities (and that changes the ideal talent profile they look for):
  - **Mature**: Well-established organizations will also likely have well-established norms, patterns, and business goals. While this environment may lack the opportunity for out-of-the-box thinking or be rigid in role scope and hierarchy, this type of organization may be more likely to invest in longer-term leadership and career development. These environments tend to prize people who can deal with complexity—multiple product lines, markets, customer segments, etc. If you're confident in your hard skills or functional expertise, this can be a good place to focus on people and leadership skills.
  - **Expansion and Scaling**: Here, the focus is on expanding the customer base, increasing market presence and maintaining competitiveness by staying ahead of the features or services needed in the next one to three years. At this stage the organization may start to focus more on bringing in specialist talent to help them better compete or build processes, service

models, etc. at scale. They may be growing from regional to national to global. This can be a good place for someone from a larger organization to help a smaller, growing organization plan ahead and organize for growth and increasing complexity.

- **Startup**: This environment is less about expertise than agility, risk-taking, and the ability to jump in and solve problems around you whenever and however they pop up. Startups tend to have a generalist view of talent skills—they want to hire smart, flexible thinkers who can do and learn to do almost anything in their field. They're looking for highly motivated people who are committed to the organization's mission and are willing to go above and beyond with the benefit of learning a broad set of skills quickly.

A lot of these nonmonetary factors you may be instinctively familiar with. You might even be at the end of this section thinking: *duh!* But have you taken the time to pinpoint where your personal sweet spot is? If you're like most of us, you haven't. Or maybe you did have your dream job all figured out, and then your personal life changed and now your sweet spot has moved. Or maybe as you've advanced in your career, you're looking for something new.

The idea here is to get the full picture of possibilities. Knowing your worth means knowing yourself and your potential. That leads to you getting more of the benefits (monetary and nonmonetary) that are worthwhile to you. When you know this, you can better choose the best type of workplace for you and signal to the people around you how they can make you feel worthwhile as well.

So time to get specific. How do you figure out what your ideal mix is with all those factors to consider? Not to fear. Where there's a will, there's a way. And I've got a way for you.

Priorities & Tradeoffs: Time. Money. Quality.

OK. So at this point, are you thinking: check, check, check—yes to all of it? Well then I've got some good news and bad news for you. Want the bad news first? Get it out of the way? Gotcha.

So bad news first. You can't have it all, all of the time. Said another way, everyone has different priorities or a different sweet spot—and so you'll trade off something less important to you to get the most important things. Life is full of tradeoffs, but they generally boil down to three categories: time, money, and quality (of experience).

Ask anyone who's moved cross-country, planned a wedding, tried to buy a house, made dinner instead of ordering in, decided to wait for a movie to stream vs. go to the theater, or just generally got on with the business of life. You with me? If you have kids, you've traded off all three—no time, no money, and no quality of life. JK. Not really. But no, kids are great.

Your job will be the same. You can have a job that's easy on the schedule, but maybe it doesn't pay as much. Or maybe it pays well, but your time is not your own. Or maybe the pay is good, but the work experience and environment (management, advancement opportunities, culture, long global hours, boring meetings teetering on tear-provoking, etc.) is not top quality in your book. There's usually something about your job that could be improved. Or even if it starts out looking perfect, you'll encounter change (example: a reorganization and new manager or re-scoped projects). But hold (drumroll), here's the good news: *That's ok.* Because you don't need everything to have your dream job. You need to have what's most important to you.

Trust me on this–your dream job doesn't equal a perfect job. Don't trust me? No problem. Let's walk it through.

1. There's no such thing as perfect.
2. Even if perfect did exist, it'd be boring (2023 *Barbie* movie plot, anyone?).
3. Think of someone you imagine has it all, and then test whether the "all" is really "all it." Likely it's not.

Let's Say Beyoncé, For Example: Beyoncé is the undisputed Queen Bey of the music industry, a beautiful woman, mother of three beautiful kids, an influential social activist, a very wealthy person, and she has tens of millions of devoted fans. But we all know Beyoncé has faced hardships throughout her life and career. She hasn't had everything she's wanted at every moment. And I imagine she's stronger, a more creative artist (see #2), and a better mother because of that. If Beyoncé makes tradeoffs (from time to time), you and I will too. Everything in life has tradeoffs.

So what makes a dream job dreamy if it's not perfect? Getting more of what you want, less of what you can live without. That's called having priorities.

Here's Another Perspective: Sam loves to travel. Sam wants to like what they do at work, but they care a lot more about having the time and space to travel—on their own, with friends, and once a year to meet up with family. After Sam spent six years building up their résumé, they got a call from a big name in their field, inviting Sam to apply for a data analytics manager position. The pay was great—18%

more than Sam's current pay. Good benefits. Sam's friends were awed. *Sam's gonna be the boss*, they cheered.

But after checking out the company and talking to a few people who worked there, Sam could see that this was a company that expected you to work while on vacation and prioritized a face-to-face presence. It wasn't worth it. Sam decided to stay with their current organization (that gave them space for travel) and focused instead on talking to their manager about other options to earn more. They worked together to outline a plan for Sam to learn a new program and help out on a project to earn that pay raise.

But let's focus on you and your priorities! So I have two questions for you: What do you want most at this point in your life? What can you do without?

Tools: Personal Career Map | **Knowing Your Worth** (Understanding Your Priorities—10-min. Exercise): Free download here: www.jomcrell.com/free

Pull out your copy of the personal career map, get a glass of your favorite bev, put on an inspirational playlist, and get ready to set the stage for your dreams.

Everybody's priorities will look a little different. That's OK. I'll give you an example of someone I know who's done a great job of getting herself in order, and it's helped rocket her career. Hopefully this example helps you think about how to use this exercise and get much closer to what's important to you.

Applause Please: My friend Maya was choosing between a couple of different job offers for a role as a learning and development trainer. One company (we'll call it: Option 1—the "Sure Thing") was offering a bigger base salary (by 10%), had a strong reputation as a mature business in her industry (real estate), and she really liked the hiring manager. The other company (we'll call it: Option 2—the "Risky Bet") was a smaller startup with a super energetic team and fun perks, like extra wellness days off, team-bonding glamping trips, etc.

Both options had positives and negatives. Because Maya was clear on her personal priorities and what she was willing to trade off, the decision ended up being easy. Her friends and parents told her to go for the Sure Thing with more money and the great boss, but for Maya, quality of experience was her top priority. She was earlier in her career, didn't have caregiving responsibilities, and was willing to trade off higher pay for more opportunity in getting a variety of experience—which is what the startup environment was likely to give her. She chose the Risky Bet, and that experience helped her move on and up to a much higher-paying role later.

Here's an example of Maya's answers for this exercise:

Step 1: Let's Explore. Use one or all of these statements to help you ID what's currently important to you.

- Because (Maya) was early in her career and prioritized learning opportunities, (she) needed to have more quality of experience and was OK with less money in (her) life.
- (Maya) wanted to get to a more senior position quickly, so right now in order to get closer to that goal, (she) needed to have more exposure to a wide variety of training programs and experiences in her field.

Step 2: Getting a clearer picture of what your priorities are? Good. Rank the three—Time. Money. Quality.

- #1 Quality #2 Time #3 Money

Step 3: Write down the top two factors for your #1 priority category that are most important.

- Key factor 1: Exposure & experience
- Key factor 2: Opportunity to experiment & own programs from start to finish

Ready for your own priorities? Alright! Get to it using your own copy of the personal career map workbook.

[Extra] Recommended Resource: *Do You: A Journey of Success, Loss, and Learning to Live a More MeaningFULL Life* by Regina Lawless

Chapter 2

Negotiate Salary & More

TLDR—Squash your anxiety around asking for a raise or negotiating a new job offer! Negotiating your worth is easier than ever, thanks to more salary transparency online. We'll break down key concepts like fair pay and cost-of-labor (because location matters!) so you can define exactly what you're worth. Plus, we'll share some killer negotiation tips and examples to get you feeling confident and ready to ask for what you deserve.

You've narrowed in on your priorities! Great! Because that's the first and MOST important step to negotiating. Now let's talk about how to negotiate. . . .

First off, I want you to know you can and should negotiate when taking a new role. Usually we think about this when signing an offer for a new role at a new organization. You can also negotiate when taking a new role within your existing organization or at times to renegotiate the terms of the role you're in.

Do you find this part a little awkward or scary? Does it leave a bad taste in your mouth? Do you wonder if what you're being offered is fair? You are *not* alone. But if you've done your homework, you can set your mind at ease that your offer is equitable and is helping you get more of what you want. Negotiating might actually be fun (or at least not horrible). Regardless, gathering resources and knowing how to negotiate will go a long way. Let's get you some of that goodness.

Do Your Research

One of the benefits of our new era of work is more transparency. There are lots of tools (like Glassdoor, Indeed, ZipRecruiter, LinkedIn, SalaryTransparentStreet, etc.) for learning about organizations from current employees. There's a lot more pay transparency too with new laws and dedicated salary comparison tools. In fact, several states have put in place (or are considering) laws that don't allow employers to ask you for pay history information AND require new job postings include pay ranges for each job[viii]. Because of this, pay transparency across the board is going up! Good stuff!

Before heading into an interview or a conversation with your current management about pay negotiation, do your research first! You will thank me! Having good data at your fingertips will make you more confident, be a great negotiating tool, and make sure you know how the offered pay package compares. Don't assume your current pay is on target for your next job. Make sure you also research what current employees say about their experience, the leadership, and the opportunities at an organization. More information = more options = better choices!

Fair Pay

You have multiple ways to check out what's fair pay for the jobs you're interested in. You can check the published salary range an organization includes with a job posting. If your state doesn't require pay transparency and it's not included in the posting, you can look online for similar jobs in a state that does require this disclosure. I encourage you to look at similar job postings anyway to get an industry-level view of your talent market from current, open listings.

Wondering exactly what a pay or salary range is? This is the low to high end of pay an organization will consider for a job type. Typically factored into the range are merit raises, cost-of-living adjustments, and bonus over time. They are often aligned with the organization's level structure. If your experience and skills are at the high end of the range, consider what your promotion or next opportunity options might be after a year or two on the job. If you're at the low end of the range, see what kind of growth opportunity and resources you have in front of you within that range.

There are also some fantastic tools online that can help you compare salaries (and typical ranges)—usually by a combination of title and location. Some will let you filter for more accurate information by double-clicking into job descriptions and adding data, like years of experience and reporting structure for the role. Some of the tools will include information on bonus, equity, or common benefits. Some favorites in order of personal preference: Salary.com, Glassdoor Salaries, Indeed, Salary Transparent Street, Monster, PayScale, ZipRecruiter. Take a look at a few of these to compare as the data can vary by field / job type. FYI: The tool's data is only as good as the number and quality of salaries that have been shared with the tool for your job type.

Location Matters

If you've ever had anything to do with real estate, you know the industry's slogan is super simple: Location. Location. Location. This matters in talent markets too. A talent market is essentially just looking at the supply vs. demand of particular kinds of talents (e.g., software engineers or teachers or HR business partners) and levels of talent (e.g., early career, mid-level, senior) in areas where an organization is operating. Location factors into the cost-of-labor that organizations use to determine salary ranges for each position.

Insider Truth: Organizations typically assess their compensation and benefits plans once (maybe twice) a year. They base these plans on cost-of-labor (NOT cost-of-living). OK, so what does that mean? Cost-of-living is something we're all instinctively aware of. It's the price of gas, rent, and how much you just forked over for that iced caramel macchiato. Where I live in the California Bay Area, we joke about how much extra we pay for our lovely, expensive sunshine.

Cost-of-labor is how much it costs to attract and retain different types of skilled professionals in certain areas. It's about how much the organization has to compete for talent where it's located. Silicon Valley is always complaining about the shortage of good engineers, so this type of labor has been well paid in the region. Oil and mineral companies are often in rural areas with a lower number of qualified workers, so they are willing to pay more to attract them to a particular location. Remote work is mixing up the cost-of-labor equation a bit. See chapter 11.

At-Will vs. Stay-Or-Pay

Generally, when you accept an offer of employment, that offer is an "at-will" employment contract. This means less job security (you or your employer can end your employment at any time), giving workers little hope of legally fighting back against actions like a layoff. But it also gives us workers the freedom to seek work on our own terms. Except in Montana, all states assume at-will employment—unless otherwise stated. More specifically, at-will means employees can quit any time with or without giving notice to their employer (DO recommend you give your employer notice—unless you're leaving for reasons of abuse). It also means an employer can use any legal reason to terminate an employee at any time.

These days some employers are using a new type of employment contract called a "stay-or-pay." This allows an employer to seek reimbursements from employees if they quit before a specified timeframe. These used to be common for senior executives or roles requiring extensive training, like airline pilots. Now employers are using them to avoid new hires ghosting them on their first day, quiet quitting (staying but doing the absolute minimum of work), and the more common trend of job hopping with shorter and shorter tenure down to sometimes just three to six months on the job. Frontline employees (nurses, teachers, drivers, etc.) are most in danger of this new tactic. These types of stay-or-pay contractual clauses go beyond traditional training repayment agreement provisions (TRAPs) used for specialized workers to repay training costs if they leave their jobs before the initial training investment period. Sometimes these contracts seek repayment that is above and beyond the salary for the role, putting workers in debt.

Don't assume. Read your offer letter carefully before signing, and if you have questions, ask. You don't want to literally end up in a TRAP, unless that truly makes sense for your work.

Defining Your Worth

Knowing your worth in a general—*Yeah, I'm all that AND more!* kind of way—is great, but not as good as knowing your worth on paper. Get your key assets, numbers, and needs locked in. This will go a long way toward giving you confidence and calm when the sweat starts to trickle during negotiations.

And don't wait to do this exercise until right before meeting your manager to talk about annual compensation raises or during an interview process. Talking about money early and often can speed your education, raise your confidence, AND help your manager get on your side. How often is often? Review your numbers and goals with yourself, your trusted network and/or manager about every three months (or each quarter).

Tools: Personal career map: **Know Your Worth** (Define Your Worth—10 min.). Free download here: www.jomcrell.com/free.

You're ready to take notes on defining your worth. Let's do this in three steps:

1. **Negotiation Assets**: Write down your key skill sets, years of experience, and education/certification level compared to the averages (both those listed in the job posting and in salary comparison tools).
2. **Ideal Salary Range**: Use those comparison points and the salary averages you researched and write down a reasonable

pay range for your job. While a published salary range in a job listing might vary by $50,000 (e.g., $65,000-$115,000), your personal pay range should center on your ideal pay number with about +/- 10% on each side (e.g., ideal = $90,000, so $80,000 [still fair]—$100,000 [good stretch]). If bonus and equity are options, put down estimates for those as well.

3. **Negotiation Needs**: Don't forget about key factors beyond the base pay! Use your top priorities from chapter 1 to make a list of the top two to three things that would help make this your dream job (beyond base pay).

Now that you're confident you know what you're worth, time to negotiate!

How to Negotiate

The first rule of negotiating is *when* to negotiate. Early in the interview process (often at the initial screening stage or "match talk"), **the recruiter or the hiring manager will ask you about salary**. This is NOT the time to start negotiating. This is simply about making sure you're both in the same ballpark so that the rest of the interview process isn't a waste of anyone's time.

Ask them to share the salary range they have for the role. If you're in a state where this is required, they must share transparently. If you're not, they may counter and ask for your current salary or the salary you want. Do NOT tell them your current salary. *It's neither here nor there*, as my grandmother would have said. This is when it's key to have your researched salary range ready. Share your range or decide if theirs is comparable.

Another possible screening stage question: many organizations will now ask you about location—specifically about their onsite, hybrid, or remote workplace policy. Post-pandemic many organizations are still wrestling with their approach to this (see chapter 11), but they will typically have some general guidance or policy. You should be ready to respond with your own commute capabilities, but avoid falling into the trap of either assuming what's in the job posting is written in stone or getting too specific too quickly.

For example, if they ask you if you can commit to coming into an office three days a week, you can either answer based on whether you're OK with hybrid in general or need to be fully remote. At the end of the day, the exact number of days per week onsite for many professionals is often negotiable—either in the offer stage or once on the job because, many times, management is empowered to manage in-office engagement at a team level. Especially for proven high performers. The more confidence they have in you, the more willing they might be to offer more flexibility. This is what some people call "back-door remote" work.

There are firm exceptions, however. Some leaders are dogmatic about this (hello, Elon Musk!) . . . tracking daily attendance through badges or security tools and mandating time onsite. Some businesses (warehouses, manufacturing, health care, education, store-front retail, laboratory-based work, etc.) need onsite work and will also have very specific policies. If you know the general policy and how strict it is, at this stage you can make a general response. If you're in the same ballpark on salary and the onsite/hybrid/remote bucket, then I wish you luck with the rest of the interview process!

A third question to watch out for is interview homework. Employers are increasingly asking candidates to demonstrate their value and skills by completing some kind of project work. While wanting to assess for skills is understandable and one sign that employers are willing to make more skills-based hires vs. pedigree hires (a good thing!), it shouldn't be a way for them to get free labor.

If the homework is assigned at the beginning of the interview process before you even speak to the hiring manager or team, this is a red flag! If the homework assignment is later in the interview process but will take considerable time and effort, this is a yellow flag. I'll offer a couple of options.

You can counter the ask. Let them know you're happy to complete the assignment and what your consulting rate is for such assignments. Again, you might need to do some quick research on what a consultant for your type of work charges per hour and estimate how much time the homework project would take. The general rule of thumb is using your base pay by hour, then multiple by two to three times. If you're not comfortable charging a consultant fee but still feel the homework assignment is excessive, you can offer a sample of prior similar work (make sure it's legal to share re: your previous employer's policies). If they insist and you feel it's excessive, then you can always say: *No, thank you.*

Pro Tip: Interview Questions You Can Ask to Evaluate a Potential Employer

They're interviewing you, yes, BUT you're also interviewing them! Besides doing research before the interview, you can use the interview process itself to better understand how a potential employer might meet your monetary and nonmonetary needs with a few questions like these:

- What does a typical day or week look like for this role? And (follow up) what helps you get work done better? What can get in your way?
- What characteristics do your best employees share? And (follow up) how do you and your best employees invest in their career development?
- For those employees with long tenure, why do you think they stay? (Or more specifically) Why do you like working here and what's the best part of your job?
- What's the culture and environment like here (do people tend to get together outside of work, is work more collaborative or independent, how formal or informal are meetings, what kinds of activities does the team do for team building, etc.)?
- What do you think are some of the best benefits of working here?
- What was the origin of this role? Is it a backfill (replacing someone who did this exact work before), a newly defined role, an adjacent role (created to divide up or complement existing work), or something else?
- What have successful employees who've had this role before done next?

- What are the most important goals for the person in this role to accomplish in the first 90 days and then first six months?
- How does this role contribute to the organization/company's overall strategy?
- I've read about the organization/company's mission, customers and products/services, but what would you say is most important for the organization/company's long-term success (for the next three years)?

Got a job offer? Knew you would. Now you have the green light to start negotiating. That way you have two advantages: 1) you have an offer in hand (you know they want you!), and 2) you have more information about the job to compare to your years of experience, education, and skill sets as negotiating assets. This is when you want to be open about what's worthwhile to you. Pop open that *Defining Your Worth* section of your personal career map and negotiate.

How to negotiate with the best of 'em:

- **Talk In Person**: Have your negotiation conversation via video, in person, or on the phone vs. in email so that it's truly a conversation.
- **Say Thanks**: Definitely start with gratitude that they've taken the time to get to know you and trusted you with an offer to join them. Show warmth and smile—nonverbal cues go a long way.[ix]
- **Start High**: Kick off the negotiation with the salary number at the top of your range. Back it up with your negotiation assets that explain why you're worth that much. (This also gives room to negotiate down *within* your range of worth.)
- **Round It Out**: Follow up with your other key negotiation needs to find out what they can offer beyond salary. Let them

know what's most important to you. You'd be surprised how many times the hiring team is anxious to close out the offer and is prepared to meet you with benefits and perks when it's in their power to do so.

- **Speak With Confidence**: Avoid words like *just, if you could,* or *I think that maybe*, and instead say *I work better when I have . . . , I've researched this number and feel confident it's a good representation of my value*, or *I'd love to know what you offer around XYZ*. If you practice with a friend first, you'll be doubly confident.
- **Come Prepared**: They'll likely ask you some sticky questions. *Do you have any other offers?* You can say (hopefully truthfully!), *I'm talking to multiple interested parties*. I suggest prepping for similar questions—for example: *If we give you the salary you're asking for, can you start immediately?*
- **Know It's Give and Take**: This is essentially the definition of negotiation. You give some; they give some. If you want more of something, they may give less of something else. But no worries, you're prepared for this because you've ranked your priorities, right!?!
- **Know You Can Walk**: Don't back yourself into a corner. This negotiation is one job. It's not the rest of your life. If they can't meet your needs, find someone who can. If you don't have the luxury of missing out on the immediate paycheck they offer, know that you can explore other opportunities down the line.

True Story: Olivia was interviewing for her third job. She'd gone through the job offer process before, but this time she was determined to get paid at the top end of the average salary range for her type of work. She was interviewing with a company she was excited about, she'd loved the people she met, and she was dreaming of ditching her old job for this more interesting one. All good. Except that when the offer came, it was low. Crap. She spent a sleepless night tossing and turning over it. *Should I counter the offer? How would I counter? How much could I counter? And why did they lowball me? Did they not like me as much as I thought?*

In the morning she decided to counter with the top salary in her range. After all, when she started job hunting and interviewing, this was her top priority. (Cheers to Olivia for sticking to her goal!) Sadly, the company recruiter got back to her later in the day saying they couldn't meet her salary goal. Was she willing to take the original number? More anxiety ensued. But in the end, Olivia decided to stick to her goal. She said, *Thank you, but no*. This was a hard hit, because not only did she love the job and company but she turned the offer down right before the holidays. Her ugly Christmas sweater felt a little less bright and cheery that year. She wondered if she was doomed to low pay her whole career.

But right after New Year's, something happened. The recruiter called her back, said they liked her enough that they'd discussed her proposed salary with the team, and decided they could raise the offer after all. She was in! She met her goal! AND she was working with a team who had double confirmed how much they valued her. Yassssss!

Pro Tip: In some cases, you may want to negotiate based on a total rewards number. Especially for startup roles or high-growth companies where equity has high value, where base salary is lower than industry average, or in more senior positions, this can work well.

For example, you can say: *My total rewards package number is $150,000 per year. How can you help me get there?* If they say, *I'm not sure we can meet that as our base salary range is only $90,000-$140,000 per year,* then ask if equity, starting bonus, or other tools in their total rewards model can help get to your total number. You may end up with something like $120,000 base salary, $15,000 starting bonus, and a $15,000 first-year equity grant that vests—but you got your number.

Salary and rewards negotiation is a gamble. You can't know for sure what you'll get, but if you know your priorities, have done your research, and try, you'll find more often than not that you get more of what you want.

These tips are centered on a new job at a new organization, but the same basics apply when negotiating a new position in your existing organization or even when renegotiating in your current role—for example: if you think you're being paid unfairly or your key needs are not being met. You can follow the same basic set of steps: do your research, know what your priorities are, be prepared by defining your worth and what questions they might ask, and practice negotiating in advance for confidence.

Insider Truth: Studies have shown over and over again that men are often valued and paid for their *potential,* while women and people of color are valued and paid for their *proven* experience.[x] Even at companies with strong People leadership that consciously bring an equity lens to the work, I've seen this happen.

Women and people of color can help themselves beat this bias by doing two things: 1) Don't share your current salary in the interview process. Instead, do your research and find out what industry average pay is for your particular location, years of experience, etc. And 2) speak to your potential in a proactive way. During interviews, you can emphasize something like: *In every role I've taken, I've shown that I can ramp (learn) quickly and grow my impact beyond the core expectations for that role in less than a year* (then give an example).

Wow! It's such a high to negotiate well and get what you want. It may not happen on the first try, but I know you can do it. Give it a little practice, and you'll be surprised at what a shark you turn out to be!

[Extra] Recommended Resource: *Forces of Good: The Superpower of Everyday Negotiation* by S. Lucia Kanter St. Amour (2022)

Chapter 3

Get Rich Sooner

TLDR—Time to get off the financial hamster wheel. Don't just work hard for a paycheck all your life. The secret is to make your money work *for you*. Find out how passive income can unlock your financial freedom. You'll be free to go after a career you love—making more (and better!) career choices!

Like the sound of this one? Yes, please! Get ready, because this doesn't just sound good, it makes your whole life easier. It'll open up your world to more choices.

Do you dream of never worrying about money again? Is the anxiety of earning enough a big part of the stress in your job? You're not alone. More than half of Americans say they're not on track to retire—EVER.[xi] Not good, people. You can do better.

So I want you to understand how you can make your money work for you. You may think I mean focusing on getting the highest-paying job you possibly can now. Totally makes sense. I mean, highly paid work is great, but not my point here. Let me explain why. . . .

Make Your Money Work for You

There are ways to make the economy do the work of earning for you. This is the magic of compounded interest. Compounded interest is when you earn interest on savings or investments, and then that additional interest is reinvested to earn more interest. This is money making money, which then makes more money.

Case in point: Let's say you start putting $1,000 each year into a savings account when you graduate (good show!). Your total career is 40 years, and at the end of that 40 years you'd have a base principal amount of $40,000, plus interest earnings of $4,159 (based on the current average national savings account rate of 0.5%) for a total of $44,159. Hmmm, after a whole 40 years, we can do better, right?!

OK, now let's say you put $1,000 each year into a S&P index fund (Standard & Poor's 500 ®—which has been the best measure of US economic performance since the 1960s). The S&P has averaged an interest rate return of about 10% for decades. So over time those invested earnings could look like this:

- 1 year later—$1,100
- 5 years later—$6,569
- 10 years later—$15,937
- 20 years later—$57,275
- 30 years later—$164,494
- 40 years later—$442,593

Wow! Are you with me? This is like a magnitude of 10x better! Now remember, you've only been putting in $1,000 each year for a total of $40,000 over your career. Now imagine if you were to save the maximum *tax-free* individual retirement account (IRA) funds allowed by the US Government as of 2024—that's $7,000 per year. After 40 years you'd have invested $280,000 of your own money and ended with a beautiful $3,379,161! Let's go higher! If your employer offers a 401K program, you can save at least $23,000 *tax-free* per year (as of 2024) for a total of $920,000 invested over 40 years, which would land you at $11,102,959!! And these limits for IRAs and 401Ks go up every year. (Not adjusted for taxes and inflation. Feel free to run your own numbers using a compounded interest calculator like one from Nerd Wallet online.)

Passive Income

This is good stuff. Having money grow without any of the daily grind needed from you to do it is fabulous! This is commonly called passive income. You don't need to do anything—be active—to make this money. I wish someone had taught me this in school. They didn't. In fact, in my twenties I didn't prioritize money at all. I was all about travel, learning new languages and cultures, and working on my passions in nonprofit.

Epiphany Moment Here: In fact, in my mid-twenties while working in nonprofit, one of the programs I was responsible for was micro-loans combined with a financial literacy and savings program. The whole point was to help my clients live above the poverty line and become financially self-sufficient. My salary (with a master's degree!) at the time was below the poverty line. Ironic, right! I wasn't saving anything for myself. And because of this, I didn't get any of that compounded interest magic in my twenties. I've been making up for it ever since (which is possible but harder). NOTE: it's never too late to start, but start NOW!

There are two secret ingredients here: 1) time—the more time you give this process, the more you make in magnitudes (difference between linear and hockey-stick graphs), and 2) a compounded interest fund—the magic place that earns more interest on interest. That's why starting earlier makes such a difference!! Now I'm not a financial expert, and I can't give you any specifics on how to budget, save, and invest your money. There are LOTS of resources out there for that (my fave is the book *Money Honey* by Rachel Richards). But understanding that there's a lot more to making money than just your base salary is a BIG part of making work *work* for you.

More Choices with Financial Freedom

My advice is to look for every way you can to make your money work for you as early as you can. Your future self thanks you for it! It could be match accounts for paying down student loan debt, retirement accounts like a 401K (through an employer), or an IRA on your own. It could be personal investments. It could through an employer-awarded stock account or ESPP program.

This often requires putting your own oxygen mask on first. What do I mean by that? I mean that earlier in your career, prioritizing earning and saving gives you a lot more leverage later in your life. The days of life-long employment (30 to 40 years at the same company!) are long gone (thank goodness!!). The economy is evolving too fast (new skills, new industries, new tools) AND many people want to evolve how they work as well. Having a nice nest egg passively earning away gives you the financial freedom in your career to follow a passion, take a break, to just do you.

This is one of the keys to loving your career. If you're trapped in a corner never making enough money, then the likelihood that your work will feel dreamy is small. Having to focus too much on money is limiting; it restricts your choices. And choice is what you want. So as soon as you start earning money, start saving it (ideally earning passive income with a compound interest earning fund!!), and give yourself the gift of financial freedom throughout your career.

Tools: Personal career map: **Know Your Worth** (Get Rich Sooner—5 min.): Free download here: www.jomcrell.com/free.

You're ready for the last fill-in-the-blank in section one.

Create a target investment dollar number for the year and convert that blank line into a high-earning part of your net worth. Kind of like a glow up for your career and financial portfolio!

Section Two

Create More Value (For Yourself & Others)

TLDR—Want to make an impact at work? Want your work to be meaningful? Not feeling like it's always easy or straightforward? You're NOT alone! In this section we'll ditch the corporate ladder and outdated advice to help you find your career sweet spot. We'll lock in on your goals, your support team, and the superpower of people skills, plus how to counter bias. Ready to leave your mark and love your work? Let's do this!

Everything about work is about creating value. Value could be lots of things—a product, service, or experience. It could be all of the above. Whatever form it takes, that value is subjective. It needs the right context for people to agree that it's valuable.

Take Water, For Example. I can buy a bottle of water from the far end of a supermarket aisle for less than a dollar, but that same bottle might be double that price at the checkout counter or be closer to $5 at an airport. I once paid $20 for a bottle of water at a concert. Seriously.

You and the work that you do are valuable. And just like that bottle of water, when you surround yourself with the right context, people will see the full value of what you can create. This section focuses on helping you create the most value you can for yourself and for those around you. We're going to get specific about what that value is so there are no surprises at performance review or contract renewal time. When you know the value you're creating, it makes it much easier to get on the same page with others. Then you won't be building your dream job alone, but with the help of your manager and the people around you. I mean, unless of course, you'd rather go it alone. No? Didn't think so. Me either.

Chapter 4

Under-Promise & Over-Deliver

TLDR—Hustle culture puts a lot of pressure on us to go faster, do more, and be the standout. Hold, please! Let's take a different approach. Set your star up to shine bright by understanding the context you're working in. Afraid you're replaceable? Don't be. By the end of this chapter, you'll know why being replaceable is a good thing.

Take Time to Adapt

Fact: The value you were hired for is potential, not proven. What?!?! Didn't you prove your worth with your résumé, during the interview process, or in your last role? I mean, isn't that why they hired or promoted you? Not quite, my friend. Applying a skill is not the same thing as generally having a skill. Why? Because every environment and organization is different. What works in some places may not work in others. Your employer is hoping you'll do well in your role, but this is a seeing-is-believing kind of thing. So from day one in any new position, they are looking for you to *prove* you can create value. Essentially, you passed a test, but now you've got to make it real.

Before you jump into the deep end of the pool, take a breather. Get the lay of the land. If your environment or job scope is new, then take some time to understand what's going on before automatically doing what you've done before to be successful. Here's what I suggest:

Give yourself space during the first three to six months learning the role (whether that's a new company or a new position within the same company), your manager, the business, and the team. Don't just learn what needs to be done and start doing it. Also take time to learn how people operate in that particular team or company environment and how your manager likes to track and deliver work. For example, find out what your manager's work preferences are—working hours, email vs. chat, live meeting updates vs. async doc—and what their pet peeves are. What's better than being the hero doing it all? Bringing others in, making them feel valuable, and building the team up. Take the time to develop relationships—both getting to know people informally and by bringing them into work projects. You know the old *walk before you run?* Yep, this is the time to walk.

Pro Tip: Giving yourself time to adapt is true even in "fast-paced environments." In fact, maybe it's even MORE important because fast-paced organizations often rely more on relationships and unwritten process and cultural norms to make decisions than slower, more bureaucratic organizations.

Feeling the pressure to deliver results yesterday? Yep, that'll happen. If you give yourself up to this pressure, you'll be in burnout land before you know it.

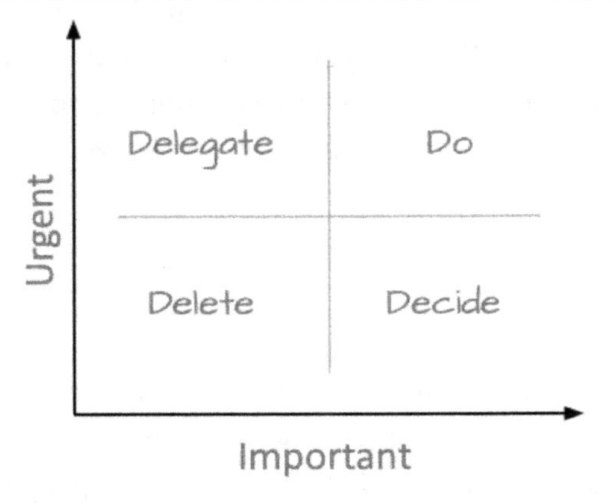

Instead create some balance for yourself from the start and use the old urgent vs. important model (a.k.a. the Eisenhower Matrix) to pace yourself. If it's urgent and important, just get it done (while seeing if others can help you get it done faster). If it's important but not urgent, this is a GREAT opportunity to learn the lay of the land and develop relationships as you go. If it's not important, then give yourself a little breathing room—delegate it, delay it for something more important, or schedule in some quick time to get it done as you go.

Don't treat everything like it's urgent!

Companies are forever talking about the *What* and the *How*. These are the two key components of how companies often review employee performance. The *What* is usually more straightforward—things like your target metrics or the project deadline and list of deliverables. Because it's more straightforward, we tend to talk more about the *What*. The *How* is more ambiguous—relationship building and influencing, work style, time management, etc. But even if they say the *How* doesn't matter (*We only care about results!*), trust me, the *How* matters, and every company, team, or manager and their *How* is a little different.

Knowing more about how things get done in your new environment or hitting that reset button and taking a fresh look at what's going on around you will go a long way. It'll make your job easier and likely make the people around you feel more appreciated. After all, you're taking the time and energy to understand their preferences. Who doesn't love that?

Act Like a Survivor

Ever seen an episode of *Survivor*? Even if you haven't (unlikely, considering it's the longest-running reality show ever—but hey, possible), you probably know what it's all about. A group of people are isolated in a place with no amenities like running water, Serta mattresses, or double lattes and need to use basic skills to survive gathering food, water, and shelter. Just as important, they don't want to get voted out by the others in the group. Have you ever noticed the winner is not the person who immediately attracts all the attention? They are not the smartest, the fastest, the best at everything. They're not the slowest, the most difficult, the loudest, and most annoying.

Middle can be a very good thing if you want to survive and win—especially in the early stages.

At work this can be true too. Drawing a lot of attention to yourself (good or bad) can also bring a lot of scrutiny. Fair or not you're setting a noticeable standard for yourself at the start without yet having all the insights and tools you might need to not just survive but thrive. Do yourself a favor and focus on surviving at first—gather the basics, do the necessary, and learn. There's likely to be more going on that meets the eye (a.k.a. don't believe in first impressions).

A Story about an Imploding Star: Kayla was a bright star. She had earned an internship at a top consulting company during college, got rave reviews from her manager and program, and from there flew through entry-level positions with a Fortune 500 to become a high-performing, first-time manager in revenue operations with praise all around in just four years. Go Kayla! Looking to make her next move, she took a management role at a Fortune 50 that paid more and promised to make her a leader in her field. She was on her way to Chief Revenue Officer!

Day one in her new role Kayla made a quick assessment. She decided she had more experience than her team, had a better handle on AI tools of the trade, and had delivered at larger scale and customer reach than what her team was currently handling. Her new manager had said, *I want you to hit the ground running*. Run she did—setting up meetings, writing a new proposal to recalibrate the spend mix for their online ads portfolio, requesting new data reports, and restructuring her team, changing role priorities.

Day 45 was a different story. Kayla was hitting roadblocks. Her team was going too slow. The latest data report hadn't come through. She was getting nervous. If these other people didn't deliver on what she asked for, how was she going to meet her new revenue targets at the end of the quarter? On top of that, Kayla's manager called a special 1:1 meeting.

The manager wasn't happy. There were complaints from Kayla's team and her stakeholders, and on top of that, they weren't seeing progress as expected. People didn't like Kayla's assumptions that she knew better. The data team couldn't prioritize her new report requests over other work. Her team felt like they never knew what to expect.

No matter how many times Kayla explained it, her manager didn't understand why she was requesting new reports or what the benefits of reorganizing her team were. Kayla was floored and frustrated. *You said you hired me because I had the expertise, could make needed changes, and that I'd have the autonomy to direct this team. That's not what you're saying now!*

By day 120 Kayla had made a fast jump to a new company and a new role. But she left with few supporters. She did go into her next job with a little more caution though. Bringing the team along, checking in with her manager to avoid assumptions, and understanding the existing processes and tools before suggesting new ones sometimes tested her patience, but definitely helped her be more successful in the end.

What does winning in the middle look like exactly? Glad you asked. Focus on understanding and delivering the core of your role—like your manager wants it done. Did you notice that last part? I said: *like your manager wants it done.* This is not the time to show off how much you know and immediately point out better ways to do everything. You likely don't yet have all the context yet needed to understand why things are done the way they are in that environment.

That doesn't mean you can't add to the equation. I'm sure you have great ideas! However, you might want to start at the beginning.

Document what your manager has asked for, repeat it back to them for confirmation with a *Yes, I can make that happen,* and then show that you can make it happen. Feel free to ask clarifying questions: *Are you recommending we do this first because it's a dependency for something later?* OR *It seems like doing this will take a while; are you open to me looking for ways to shorten the process?* Make sure you're writing down the steps you've taken to deliver whatever it is that you've agreed on. Then accomplish a little extra. Deliver it a little faster than agreed. Or help a coworker with their project on the side. Or find a way to save the team some money. Once you've done that, you're *proven*. Now you can take off your seatbelt. You are free to move about the airplane and takeoff for great things!

Tools: Personal Career Map | Create Value (Under-Promise and Over-Deliver—5-min. exercise): Free download here: www.jomcrell.com/free

Pull out your copy of the personal career map, flex your muscles, and channel your best boss vibes.

For this exercise, you're going to take notes on your manager's (and organization's) top goals for you with the one to three things you need to do in the next three to six months to deliver on that goal.

Now that you've proven you can create value on your manager's terms, you will have the trust and street cred needed with your team to introduce your own ideas, ways of doing things, etc. You can step up with confidence and spend some time leaning into your expertise and passion, building and learning, stretching into new projects, and all the things that create value for you and your team. Before long, you'll be asking yourself, *So what's next?*

Be Replaceable

Yep, you're replaceable, and that's a *good* thing. Someone else can and will take your role and do well in it. This is something you want to happen—eventually. Otherwise, you'd be stuck in the same role, level, and salary forever. Ugh. No thank you, right? We want to move on and up!

Once you've got the basics of your role down—you're comfortable, you understand how things work, and your manager agrees—you should be looking at what's next. After all, you've proven you can create the value needed (and more hopefully) for that role. This is the time to focus on your future, so don't spend time "protecting" your current role. Have a coworker who's "encroaching" on your projects? Try saying this: *Tori seems to have some good ideas and energy for this work. I'm open to that, if they want to give it a try. That would free me up to (insert something you'd like to do that will take you onward and upward).*

So what IS next? Do you know? Have it all planned out? Not quite? No worries. Let's talk about that. Cue: next page, chapter 5.

Chapter 5

Get Specific about What's Valuable to You

TLDR—Feeling like your dreams are just . . . dreams? New Year's resolutions #fail anyone? Been there. But achieving your goals isn't just about wishful thinking. This chapter is about making your goals reality. Going for the ultimate win? When your goals align with your manager's priorities—that's the sweet spot! And because life throws curveballs, let's go over some pro tips to handle changes, even layoffs, and stay on track. Get ready to make an impact!

Make Your Goals Come True

If you try, you risk failure. If you don't, you ensure it. I don't know who originally came up with that quote, but it's all over Instagram, Pinterest, YouTube, and all the places we post the inspirational quotes we hope we're living up to. Well friend, this is the chapter where we make it real for you. We're going to get specific about creating more value for yourself so that you're not only trying; you're living your best work life.

What I'm talking about here is setting and reaching your goals. You've done this before—be healthier, get more sleep, dry January, make it through all five seasons of *Stranger Things*, clear some more shelves in the closet, spend less on lattes. . . . So you also know that sometimes you can make it stick, and sometimes that goal goes out the window. Apparently 92% of us don't achieve our New Year's goals.[xii] There are so many reasons for that kind of fail rate—exhaustion at the end of the work week, hanging with friends who don't share your goals and (unintentionally) encourage you to break them, competing priorities . . . and sometimes life just gets in the way.

In fact, goal failure has been studied so much that the reasons we don't succeed are pretty consistent and clear: we make our goals too hard, we're not passionate enough about them (they aren't our true priority), we don't track our progress, we don't have support to complete them, and we don't give them enough focus. Good news! Since we know why we often don't reach our goals, we can design our goals to make sure we do succeed.

I like to keep it simple. Google "goal setting" and you'll find countless articles offering advice. All good stuff, but it's usually a bit long and complex. I recommend an easy three-step way to set successful goals.

1. Get specific.
2. Make it timebound.
3. Share your goals.

Yep. It can be this easy. The experts and my own experience (based on plenty of mistakes as well as some wins) tell us goal setting is most successful when you do these three things. Depending on the research you look at, doing each of these things separately can increase your chances of success by 14-45%. Doing these three together can increase your success by 95%.[xiii] Regardless, the only way to successfully meet your goals is to take action on them. Cause wanting something to happen without taking action is a wish. I don't know about you, but wishing my way to career success doesn't sound like a solid plan. So let's talk about how to make your goals come true.

Get Specific

With work, there are two sets of goals we need to think about: your organization's or manager's goals and your goals. In chapter 4 we talked about understanding, writing down, and checking in on your organization's goals for you via conversations with your manager. A reminder: the keywords here are *writing* and *checking in*. You want to get to your performance review with no surprises. If you write down your manager's goals for your role and regularly check-in on the steps you're taking to reach them, you're saving your own sanity (no *say-wha?* moments), covering your a$$ (that's what we call CYA in the business), and avoiding recency bias (so your manager doesn't forget all the great stuff you did many months ago). But throughout that process, you'll also have made those goals more specific (by writing down the steps you're taking to achieve them), kept them timebound (by committing to getting them done before the end of the project or your review project), and shared those goals (with your manager and your team).

Now you want to give your own personal goals the same benefits—if not better! Let's set your own goals for work and make sure you reach them. So step 1—get specific. Let's practice with an example.

> **Pro Tip:** Don't neglect your core work while working on your personal goals! (Note: your core work is what your manager prioritized and you agreed to do.)

Let's take a common New Year's resolution example—exercise more. Yeah, that'd be good. Set that one myself. But I didn't stick with it and neither did most people who set that goal. Why? Too vague. What kind of exercise? How often? What will get better if I exercise—will I look better, feel better, be stronger? OK. So let's be specific about what I really want.

New Year's Goal: I want to be able to walk my dog up the very steep slope to my house without huffing and puffing. This is because I love my dog AND have to walk him every day (twice! Ruff!). It's also because I want to feel healthier.

OK, so now I've got a specific goal that helps me with both things I want. Is that enough? No. Sadly. This is still not specific enough.

Let's try again.

New Year's Goal (Take 2): I want to be able to walk continuously at a fast pace (hey, sometimes it's raining!) and make the walk at least 20 minutes. That gives puppy time to do his thing—thing one and thing two—and it's what's recommended for a minimum of daily exercise for us humans to feel healthier.

Oh yeah, now that's a challenging goal but still easy enough to know if I'm making the grade. It's a good level of specific. And I know that if I make this goal, I can always raise the challenge and do better. I'm all in on the #hotgirlwalk trend—even if the only thing that's hot is my red face climbing back up the hill.

Back to Work Goals and another Example: I'll start with the most common career goal I hear—to get promoted. First, there are a few challenges with that goal.

1. (Not in your control) Promotion is a decision made by your department leaders, not you.
2. (Not actionable) This goal doesn't help you decide what to do next.
3. (No specific value identified) What value will you get from being promoted? To make more money, for the prestige, to become a "leader," to work on more exciting projects, to meet your parents' or significant other's expectations? Are you sure you know what you really want?

What's the first step to the career growth you want? I can't emphasize this enough—**knowing what you value** and want to achieve. Trust me, if you're not specific about your goals, someone else will set them for you. Then you're working for their goals and values, not yours. And, I'm not talking necessarily about more money here, but experiences, skills, connections, etc. These are the things that make the time you spend working more fun, interesting, and/or help you get where you want to go next.

Remember that little stat about working 90,000 hours in your lifetime? You'll have lots of time to invest in work. Thinking it's too much? Yeah, burnout is real. Not excited about the idea of a "job" at all? I hear you. But what if you thought about your job, or more accurately your work, as a way to get what you want next? What if it's a way to test out and build value that you could apply to a passion project, your side hustle, building your own company, or getting the position you've always dreamed about? What if you thought about the work you're doing as an opportunity to satisfy your curiosity, to make meaningful connections, to learn something that creates value for you and people you care about? Suddenly work isn't a place we go to or a paycheck or a thing we have to do; it's a way to make your life more fulfilling.

We talk a lot these days about following your passion. I'm all for it! But (flashing alert siren!) if you're not specific about what your passion is, what actions bring your passion to life, and how to tap into your work environment, network and skills to fulfill your passion, then you might just find yourself exhausted, feeling tricked, or isolated in your work. Big ugh. I've been there. I feel you.

I see so many people looking to their employer to fulfill their sense of purpose and passion. Millennials—yep, you know what I'm talking about. Employers caught on to the Millennial desire for purpose-driven work, and they have been more than happy to refresh their websites and candidate pitch decks to sell their own version of mission-, purpose-, and passion-driven work. Many employers overpromised and under-delivered on this one. They obviously didn't read chapter 4. That miss has definitely helped contribute to where we are now—all-time lows in employee engagement and company loyalty.[xiv]

There's also a growing feeling (especially among Gen Z, who watched this story fall apart) that work has become transactional. In fact, more than half of workers today think of their work relationship as transactional—just collecting a paycheck. The pandemic refocused so many people on all the things in life that are more important than work.[xv] And Gen Z as a group rightly rejects so much of the long-held rigidity that had defined work before then. We are learning (finally!) that work doesn't need to be done in a particular place, between particular hours, wearing particular clothes, by people who look and speak a particular way.

As meaningful as these changes are to the world of work, it'll take some time for everything to catch up and balance out. In the midst of that confusion, being clear about what's valuable to you is a very steadying asset.

Truly understanding what your priority is, or where the value is, is key. Not quite sure? No worries—go back to *Priorities and Tradeoffs* in chapter 1 and the first section of your personal career map. Reground yourself in what's truly worthwhile to you, and then come back here for next steps.

Once you have a clear priority, ask yourself a couple of questions to understand what can help you move toward making that an achievable goal:

- What motivates you about your work and will help you grow in the direction you want to go?
    - Examples: learning, specific types of projects, building relationships, mastering a tool or technology, owning a project end-to-end to practice delegation, etc.
- What actions can you take now to do more of that?
    - Examples: volunteer, take on a side project, put extra effort into a current project on the part you most value, take a course in your area of interest, shadow someone doing what you're interested in.

Let's Go Back To That Promotion Goal: My friend Marissa told me she wanted to get promoted next cycle. She was so frustrated her manager was not more encouraging and didn't understand why her company wasn't interested in her growth. I asked her why promotion was the answer, and we had an interesting deep dive into her work life for 20 minutes.

Turns out that she had two problems driving her goal for promotion: 1) she was getting kind of bored with her work and was thinking about moving on—internally or to another company, and 2) she worried that other people were getting more attention from leadership and she was getting left behind. Now that level of detail we could work with!

After talking it through, Marissa got more specific about her goal. She decided to seek out a high-profile stretch project that would get her more visibility, be more interesting for her, and she wanted to work on it before her next performance review came around in four months. She knew her department was working on a merger and acquisition (M&A), and as those projects are intense, M&A teams are usually looking for volunteers. This was her chance to try something new, take something heavy off her manager's plate, and work with new people.

Now let's focus on your goals and get specific about what you want!

Tools: Personal Career Map | Create Value (Get Specific—10-min. exercise): Free download here: www.jomcrell.com/free

Pull out your copy of the personal career map, refill your water bottle, put on an energy-driving playlist, and get ready to get specific about a goal that's top value to you.

For this exercise, write your goal down and note the specific types of skills, experiences, connections, and/or tools that will help you get there.

When you've got that down, let's picture your success. Imagine you're on the other side and your goal is a win! It feels good to look back and see how far you've come. I knew you could do it! (Crowd roaring!) Live in the moment for a bit. What's making you so happy when you imagine your success? No matter what challenges came up, why was completing this goal so valuable? Use that thought to fill in the vision headline prompt.

Did you know that taking the time to actually envision your success makes it much, much more likely to come true? It's a technique called visualization, and it's been helping leaders and entrepreneurs get to the top and build their businesses for years. There's no reason that you can't bring that visualization power to your goals too.

For my friend Marissa, here's what part 3 (Get Specific) would look like:

Get Specific

- Goal: *Take on a stretch project with high visibility before my next performance review*
    - Skills: *Project management & delegation*
    - Experiences: *Work with the M&A team*
    - Connections: *More visibility with my director & the head of product legal*
    - Tools: *Apply AI to learn how to create better prompts for project summaries & research*

- (Visioning Headline) No matter what, I got *an interesting project, powerful new connections for my network & AI skills that will make all my work easier* and that was worth it.

Got your own goal summary filled out? Great job on getting specific!

Make It Timebound

OK. Now lock that goal into a three- to six-month plan. Create milestones to check in with yourself on how it's going. Doing this means you'll have broken down your goal into yummy, bite-sized, actionable steps that can be measured for success. I recommend weekly milestones since this seems to make it more likely for people to reach their goals, and it aligns with the cadence of the work week. Regardless, give yourself the satisfaction of checking off boxes as you go. If you need to pivot along the way, do that. This is your goal, your plan. You own your success.

Let's see what Marissa's doing to make her specific goal timebound. A little research told her that delegation skills are what they're looking for at the next level, and she wants to get better at this. So she created a plan that included listening to three expert podcasts about delegation, shadowing someone at work who's known for doing this well, and volunteering to lead her team's portion of an M&A project that would require this skill over the next three months. Her timeline included some types of milestones that might be useful in your plan:

- **Initial Phase:** Setting up milestones, identifying resources, doing research, and raising a hand for this opportunity

- **Middle Phase:** Following through on those podcasts, getting buy-in on and executing her project plan, taking notes on what she was learning, collecting feedback, and probably making some pivots (adjusting based on what she learned along the way)
- **Final Phase**: Giving credit to the people involved / who helped her, finalizing her notes on what she learned (both wins and opportunities, great for her performance review write-up), making sure her project was completed according to the success metrics set for it, and updating her resume

Your own milestone list for your goal may look different. That's OK. The main thing to keep in mind here is to break your goal down into doable "bite-sized" work, celebrate wins as you go, and use those milestones to reflect and pivot as needed.

Pro Tip: People often fail to see their goals through because they don't make the time for it. I'm not talking about adding one more thing to your list of everything to get done. That's the problem. If your goal is just one more thing you've got to do, then you haven't really prioritized it.

Since this goal is directly linked to your priorities (from section one), then you know it's really important to you. That means you're good to trade something else off your list—something lower priority. Do that and make more space for what you truly want.

A Great AND Painful Example: Here's what can happen when you haven't truly locked in on your priorities. Let's talk about Alicia. Alicia was a success story. She had fast tracked her career—moving from intern to head of product management in only 12 years. She was making a great salary with fantastic benefits. She'd had two children during that time. She and her wife bought a home and brought in a designer to make it into their dream house. She was living the dream, right? Or was she?

Because Alicia was also fried. She told me about taking meetings during her commute, all day, and after she got home while she was picking up the kids and getting them dinner. She had started to hate her job, which was no longer about customer connection and design but about managing urgent problems, herding cats, politics, and dealing with what seemed like a constant revolving door of people coming and going on her teams. She didn't want to overwhelm her wife with work talk all the time, but she felt so lonely, like she didn't have a true confidante to help her sort it all. She started to cry when she told me about feeling like she never slept.

She was successful. She'd made it. Why wasn't she happy? When I asked Alicia what was most important to her and what she was willing to trade off, she couldn't answer. She was terrified at the idea of letting something go. She was adamant: *"It's all important."* She was overwhelmed. So instead we started by identifying the biggest time sink in her week.

She told me she was spending multiple meetings each week and often time at night managing "urgent requests and emergencies." She felt a lot of pressure to solve these problems and knew her boss appreciated her keeping them off his plate. But it was a lot of time and meant she virtually had no boundaries between her personal life and work. We talked about how she could engage her team leads to better handle these situations. Turns out, when she openly talked to them about it, they admitted they were also losing sleep over these urgent requests and thought it was impacting team morale. They worked together to better define "urgent" vs. "important," reestablish priorities with their partner teams, and set up a plan for solving and escalating these types of problems. Within a few weeks urgent escalations went down by 80%, the team was much happier, and Alicia suddenly had more time and sleep.

After solving that problem, Alicia was in the right mindset to talk priorities. Ultimately, she felt she wasn't learning anymore and missed the more direct connection to the product-management work that she'd loved in the first place. She wanted to focus on quality of experience. She decided to give her team leads opportunity for more responsibility in some of the areas she wanted to back away from. Instead she would spend more of her time deep diving each quarter on one or two projects where she played an active role with the team. Because she carefully talked to her team first and matched their interests with the work she was trying to balance, they were really receptive. Working first-hand with the team also helped her observe the day-to-day and then work with her leads on ideas to improve their hiring and team-building approach.

Alicia learned the hard way that getting more of what you want means being willing to give up something you can live without. Once she opened up to that possibility and focused on her priorities, she got double the benefits. She was happier AND she made the people around her happier.

Sometimes we're so focused on an idea of success that we trade off what's most important to us. Often we try to do everything. That's definitely a recipe for burnout. But even more than that, it's a recipe for failure. Your priorities and goals need space to grow. Make sure you make time for what's important to you.

Tools: Personal Career Map | Create Value (Make It Timebound—15-min. exercise): Free download here: www.jomcrell.com/free

Let's go back to your personal career map to break down your goal over the next three to six months.

Before you get writing, take a moment to take a deep breath and think of three things you're proud you accomplished. That's better. Now you're in the right mindset for this exercise.

Once you've got your milestones set, I bet you're ready to get started. But don't dive in quite yet. There's one more step for making your goal come true.

Share Your Goals

Made it this far? Great work! But why work alone when you can get something done with people supporting you? Tell people what your goals are (and what you're accomplishing). This is not about boasting but to learn and get help—so don't be shy. Research tells us that sharing goals makes them more likely to come true. Telling other people helps them keep you accountable for what you said you wanted to do, and it means you'll have people checking in to cheer you on. Good stuff!

So who should you share your goals with? Gather your very own "board of advisors"—or three to five (no more than ten) positive professionals who you respect or look up to—and tell them what you're trying to accomplish. Being on an organization's board of advisors is usually a paid and prestigious role because of how valuable this group is to the organization's decision-making and future planning. Why shouldn't you have your own board of advisors for your career? They can help open doors, coach, share resources, make introductions, help hold you accountable, etc. These are the people who will advocate for you when you're not in the room. Out of your larger network connections, you can include a variety of personal and work relationships in your own board of advisors:

- **Peer**: Someone you feel comfortable talking with and who can offer you an alternative perspective.
  - Not all mentors need to be senior to you, but make sure you're not spilling dirt or confidential information with a peer at the same organization.
- **Friend**: Someone who knows you well, including your strengths, habits, weaknesses.

- This should definitely be someone outside your organization.

- **Senior Leader:** Someone with more influence and experience than you.
    - If within your same organization, great, but can also be a mentor from outside.
    - If you're seeking a promotion, a senior leader from your same department can help advocate for you during the promotion process.
- **Role Model**: Someone who's doing the work today that you're interested in for your future.
    - Like that job-shadowing mentor we talked about in Marissa's example or someone outside your company.
- **Social Network Connection**s: Someone you've maybe never worked with or know well, but you both share interests or the same type of job.
    - LinkedIn is a great place to meet people like this, and they're also great for things like pay comparisons.
- **Your Manager**: Ideally your manager is someone who helps champion you.
    - At the least they should be aware of your personal work goals so that they aren't surprised and feel that these goals are getting in the way of the core work they hired you for.
- **Family or Friend**: Someone you live with or talk to on a regular basis who provides more of that day-to-day support.
    - Word is that this type of relationship is especially effective in keeping you accountable.
- **Paid Advisor**: Coaches are not a substitute for the value of other members of this group, but they can help you better

understand yourself and get the most out of the relationships with your board of advisors.

- There are lots of options today, from life coaches to career coaches in standalone practices or via platforms like BetterUp, The Grand World, and Medley.

I recommend including someone in your board of advisors group who is from the same background or identity group—someone you're truly comfortable with. Someone you can get real with. I also recommend including someone who is different—different background, gender, approach to work, etc. Different experiences and perspectives offer you a wider range of support. Finally, all relationships work best when they are mutually beneficial. As you form your board of advisors and curate those relationships, find ways to give back.

Tools: Personal Career Map | Create Value (Share Your Goal—5-min. exercise): Free download here: www.jomcrell.com/free

Hop back over to your personal career map and jot down the names of your new board of advisors. Maybe have a couple of backup options because someone might be tapped out at the moment in their own life. No worries, you'll have options.

Great. Well done! Take a moment to sit back and glory in having created a group of people who are cheering for your success!

Find the Sweet Spot

Now you've got the two things you need most to be successful in your role. You've got a clear understanding of what your manager wants. AND you've got personal goals that are meaningful to you. You know where the sweet spot is? Right in between.

What's better than a WIN-WIN? Nothing. When you can build a bridge between what both your manager and you most want to accomplish that means everything you do is worth double. Points for you and points with your manager.

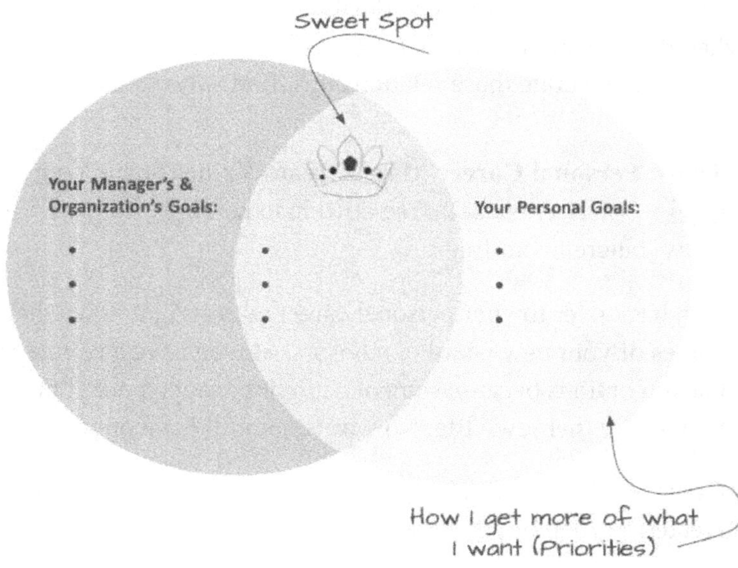

When your work meets both sets of goals, then, yeah, the crown is yours.

You're ready for action. First, I highly recommend setting up or using an existing 1:1 meeting with your manager to talk about your goal. Tell them you're confident in your ability to do your current core work well (yes, right?) AND are excited about continuing to learn and develop. Remember, no surprises! I'd like to think that your manager would see this as a plus—that you're motivated, learning, upskilling.

Still, if the idea of this conversation sets off alarm bells, well, I understand. You can obviously work on a personal work goal outside of your day-to-day job and without telling your manager or team. If this is the path you take, just be aware that if your manager learns about your new work project from someone else, they may not be super happy.

Pro Tip: Now you're ready to reach out to each member of your board of advisors. Give them the summary of what you hope to accomplish by when, and then ask if they'd be willing to give you some advice and check in to keep you accountable to your goal.

Some great lead-ins to ask for advice?

- Have I left anything out?
- Have you done something similar, and if so, what did you do to make sure you met your goal?
- Do you have any resource or tool recommendations you think would help me with this goal?
- Do you know anyone who's really good at what I'm trying to do? Would you be willing to introduce us so that I can learn more?
- Is there anything I can do for you (share experiences, support, connections)?

Now it's time to get going on your plan—starting with your first milestones. Nothing like checking off some boxes to get a nice dopamine hit.

And here's the biggest win. Even if you don't get that promotion this particular round, you learned something valuable that will serve you well. On top of that, achieving a goal will boost your confidence . . . and plenty of career coaches say that confidence in itself can be a huge differentiator. AND now you have supporters who not only know you are goal-oriented but that you can work toward a goal and make it happen. This is just the starting point to great things happening.

Handle Change like a Pro

What if you're rockin' along, checking off those milestones, and then, BAM! You get one of those long, tedious emails explaining that your team is being reorganized. Or you get sick and you're down for the count for a whole week straight. Or your team member suddenly announces they're leaving for another job, and you're asked to take on some of their work.

Yep, change happens. And the way the world is spinning these days, change happens frequently. Lots of things are fluctuating and hard for businesses to pin down, let alone us as individuals—macroeconomics, supply-chain disruptions, war, climate-driven disasters, global capital flows or how money is invested, talent-market shifts, generational shifts in consumer demand, new technology like GenAI . . . take your pick. There are lots of reasons that change in our work environments is a constant.

Will this affect us? Definitely. But we don't have direct control over any of that macro stuff. And trying to direct what you don't have control over is an exercise in burnout. Not only that, but it uses up energy you could be directing toward the things that are in your control.

If you keep your personal career goals focused on what's in your control (your interests, time, energy, and investment), then you will always come out ahead. When you have the full picture of the choices available and you've made the choice of how to focus your personal career map, you're in control. You can pivot, persist, or plan your way to the things that have the most value to you.

Back to Marrisa's Story: Marissa learned this lesson. Halfway into her M&A stretch project, the whole thing hit the brakes. The M&A negotiation didn't succeed, and the two companies decided not to complete the acquisition. $hit. But Marissa was determined to get something out of this project, so she pivoted while keeping her specific goals in mind.

She decided to use all the work put into building out the acquisition plan so far to create a playbook for any future M&A project involving her function. She used GenAI to help summarize that information and research some of the gaps that would have been part of the completed acquisition plan. She reached out to other key project stakeholders with specific questions to help her fill in other gaps in her playbook (delegation win!). She then presented her playbook to her manager (after giving them a first pass—no surprises!), director, and head of product legal. Finally she wrote a thank you post to everyone in the project and shared her playbook link. Talk about good vibes all around! Go, Marissa!

A Personal Pivot: My own goal (walking the dog at a fast pace for 20 minutes to get healthier and not huff and puff it up the hill to my house) is a little less inspirational but also a good pivot story.

Wouldn't you know it, but about three weeks after getting on my new walk routine, I got a killer flu. Took me out for almost two weeks. That first walk after was brutal. Sob. I cried real tears I was so tired and defeated. Seemed like not only were the first three weeks of my #hotgirlwalk wasted but I was even more out of breath. Damn flu.

Getting the flu was not in my control. Seriously. I got it from my loving husband. Unfortunately, we share pretty much everything. There was no avoiding it. But reaching my goal was still in my control. I just pivoted a little. I let myself slow the pace—as long as I kept moving . . . sometimes at a crawl. I started wearing a lightweight mask to keep my throat warm after being raw from coughing up a storm. I got one of those water belts serious runners wear. I looked like an over-geared idiot, but I worked my way back up to my goal in (applause, please) two weeks.

OK, Let's Talk About One of the Most Traumatic of All Work Changes—The Layoff. Layoffs happen. It's incredibly rare to meet a working professional who hasn't been laid off at some point in their career. I've laid people off, and I've been laid off. Heck, I had to lay myself off once. But that doesn't make it feel normal or easy. In fact, it can feel like the ultimate cancel move. It's scary, damages self-esteem, and creates unease—*could it happen again?* Layoffs are so hard to digest because they are business decisions outside of your control, but they impact you in a very personal way—your financial security, sense of respect, your daily routine and structure. A layoff can make your whole life feel like it's spinning out of control.

So I've got some specific advice about coming back from a layoff:

- **Exit gracefully** or as gracefully as you can.
    - In the moment when we're first notified, we're likely to say something we'll regret; instead you can simply

say something like: *I understand. I'll take time to review my severance agreement to see if I have any questions.*

- **Give yourself space** to process.
    - Take a week or so to let yourself run through the emotions.
- **Focus on what's essential** to be supported and healthy.
    - Note: there is no shame in filing an unemployment claim and seeking public assistance—you paid tax dollars to support you at exactly this time.
- **Review the severance package** before you sign.
    - Take time to understand what questions you have and double check that the package is truly fair according to state laws and common practice.
- **Remind yourself** that your now-former employer is only one of many sources of value.
    - Your network, your skills and past experiences, your personal goals, and your potential to create more value in other work opportunities are all still there!
- **Reflect on what's next** because it doesn't have to be the same.
    - Do you want to pursue the same career path or is this an opportunity to pivot to something that's higher priority for you?
- **Practice explaining** that you were laid off.
    - This will help you stay matter-of-fact and strong in interviews AND fend off those tactless but well-intended questions from the aunt who always gives you an ugly sweater for the holidays.

You got this! Go back to your personal career map and see the proof of your value. You already have what you need: Priorities. Skill sets.

Experiences. Connections. Goals. If there's something in this mix you need to add, revisit or repair—you can do that. One employer doesn't control these things. You own them. You have what you need to move forward and make your next work opportunity your dream job.

[Extra] Recommended Resource: **Pathmatch** (focused on Gen Z and the college-to job-market transition but can also be an interesting way to more generally explore your skills and types of job opportunities)

Chapter 6
See the Value in Others

TLDR—Relationships can be tricky. But since work is a collaborative exercise, let's decode the people skills you need to make your work relationships valuable and a positive source of energy. We'll figure out the "unwritten rules" of work culture, tackling challenges like imposter syndrome, codeswitching, office politics, and bias. We'll cover how to master core or universal people skills that help us adapt to today's more distributed workplaces (think communication and showing up).

People Skills Are #1

I love that we spent time getting to know your worth and how you can create value for yourself. It's so important. Fill your own cup. Put on your oxygen mask first. Know your worth. Now you're ready for others. That's good because finding and amplifying value in other people is critical to making work worthwhile.

Einstein said, *"Focus on being valuable, not being successful."* He was a pretty smart dude by all accounts, and I think he was right about this. Success is an outcome. Creating value is the work you do to get to success. And the work we do is all in the context of understanding the needs of, working with, and delivering value to other people—whether that's our coworkers, customers, partners, or any other stakeholder. Making others feel valued is an amplifier for your own career. People will champion you, open doors, excuse your faults, respect your ideas, and add to your success if they feel valued by you.

With GenAI sucking most of the air out of the #futureofwork conversation, I wouldn't blame you if you thought digital skills were your number one asset. Definitely digital skills have been, are, and will be an asset (see chapter 13). And you definitely need "hard skills"—the functional expertise you bring to your work, like delivering services, strategic planning, program design, or organizing data. They are the foundation for the type of work you'll do. But they are not your number one skill set. People skills are.

Across different industries, company types, and role types, lots of studies from the likes of McKinsey, Deloitte, Georgetown University Center, and sooooo many more researchers[xvi] find that more and more employers are prioritizing people skills (also known as "soft skills," but I kinda hate that term). In fact, as technology automates and augments or helps us more quickly perform our hard skills, workers who stand out will be the ones with solid people skills. More importantly, people skills are a top asset in helping you find more opportunities and creating the best context for your dream job.

Insider Truth: Meritocracy doesn't exist. We like to believe it does—the idea that if we work hard someone will notice. That we'll get promotions based on a fair assessment of our abilities. We SHOULD continue to strive for fair, unbiased reviews of each other. But pure merit rarely wins the day. While the HR or People Team can put processes and checks and balances into place to mitigate bias, it cannot change human nature.

To help fill the gap, workers need to put their own mitigation measures in place—and polishing up your people skills is a great way to do that. Good people skills help you advocate for yourself, build a supportive network, and combat bias. Look for more on how to do this throughout the book.

Still not buying it? Or not loving the idea that you're dependent on other people to create value for yourself? Take a moment to think about the people you appreciate most. I bet they don't make you feel useless, stupid, cheugy (thank you Gen Z for this oh-so-fun-to-say slang), boring, unworthy, ghosted, and they don't throw shade at you every chance they get. Am I right? Work is so much more dream-like when we value the people we work with—and they value us.

So what are these people skills? Does this mean I have to be everyone's bestie? And can't people skills vary from organization to organization? It's true that every organization has its own culture and norms. This is often what people mean when they talk about the "unwritten rules" of the workplace. But it's also true that there are core people skills valuable everywhere. And no, it doesn't mean you have to be "friends" with everyone at work. So let's talk about both: the core people skills that will help you no matter where you go, and the people skills prioritized in each unique organization. And while we're at it, let's talk about some common barriers to making sense of all this.

Unwritten Rules & Imposter Syndrome

Feel like a fraud? Thinking you don't have what it takes? Imposter syndrome is something most of us suffer from at some point. And this feeling can be an extra big challenge, especially when we're trying to learn those unwritten rules unique to each organization.

While a pretty common way to fight back against imposter syndrome, I'm not a fan of the fake-it-til-you-make-it approach. I think this has some dangerous assumptions in it. If you have to "fake it," how do you know what "making it" really is? Are you throwing too much of your true self out in order to adopt some other vision of success? We often do this because we're afraid of not being taken seriously or making mistakes in a new environment. That's legit. Feeling uncertain in a new environment is OK. But, instead of acting out of fear, I encourage you to give yourself time to observe what's going on around you. This also keeps you from looking too thirsty and desperate to impress. Find the best examples of behavior in the people around you and take your cue from that. Find the people who are confident, good at finding solutions or moving work forward and who also know how to uplift others. That's a good way to quickly learn the best people skills that will ensure you make it in your new environment.

What can you do in the meantime? Allow your best self to shine through. Do some prep before meetings—read up, write down some questions, or ask a coworker what's typically expected. Be engaged. Listen, nod, and take notes. You don't have to be the loudest voice in the room to impress. If you have something to add, great. But maybe start with a question first—like: *Is that something we've been successful doing before?* This shows that you're listening to others—as well as contributing your own ideas. Some of the most inspiring leaders I've seen in action led with quiet confidence. They listen to what everyone else says in a meeting before speaking up, and then what they raise is additive while reinforcing the value of what they've heard from others. Worried you'll be underestimated? Good. All the better when you surpass their expectations next time.

And it's not just official work time that's important. Taking time to hang out with people in informal moments is key. I'm not talking about earning a reputation as top gossip or having so much fun at the company holiday party that you end up drunk and wondering what you said to who. No. Definitely not advising that. I'm talking about scheduling in coffee chats, showing up to celebrate coworkers' birthdays (whether you like 'em or not), and joining the boss when they invite people to a Happy Hour, or even better, a Wellness Hour. These informal moments are great trust builders and help people see you as a human—which buys you space and grace. It's also a great time to get more information on office politics—who you can count on, who you should avoid. AND it's another great time to advocate for yourself . . . in a casual way.

Imagine you run into your manager's manager at a Wellness Hour. After some chitchat, they say something like: "*How do you like it here?*" Opportunity alert! With your priorities nailed and your goals in mind, you say: "*Loving it! I really like doing X work and could see myself stretching a bit to do Y work. Have any recs for how I could do more of that?*"

You'll find your own way to show up in your new work environment. Whatever gives you confidence, lean in. What doesn't, lean out. Just don't feel the pressure to know all the rules immediately.

Insider Truth: Internal mobility is a term used to describe different types of opportunities for job opening, role moves, stretch assignments, etc. inside an organization. Most companies do not have a good process or system for advertising them to employees. Sometimes this is because of technical complications. Internal job board tools are not so great. Sometimes it's because leaders prefer to "handpick" people and don't really want to open a role up.

Regardless, being connected and having a good internal network at multiple levels in your organization is key to accessing more opportunities. And investing in informal connections greases the wheels, as well as making it much more likely you hear about these opportunities in the first place.

There's another dynamic to imposter syndrome that can affect us—code switching. This is when you feel the need to adjust your language, appearance, or behavior to fit into the norms around you. Most of us need to code switch at some point. If you're in marketing and you're presenting to a group of techies, you'll be more successful if you adapt how you show up—and vice-versa. If you're meeting with partners from a more formal business environment, you might need to throw a blazer on over your tee shirt and jeans. If you have several introverts on your team, you might need to reign in your exuberant extroversion to give their voices space.

For some people code switching can be an always-on, every interaction exercise. Maybe that's because the cultural norms at your workplace feel like they're running over your identity norms. This often happens in cases where there is a dominant group and minority groups—for example: race or gender representation (being the only one), coming from a different country and culture, or being neurodivergent. If this is your situation, you can still give yourself some choices and control over how you show up. But first off, if you need to leave a toxic environment, go—don't make yourself miserable if it's not working. If you think the positives outweigh the challenges, here are some possible tactics:

- **Find your circle**: Whether it's one or two people or a whole community like an employee resource group, your circle or community can give your identity safe space and support, and they may have suggestions on how to better navigate the norms of your work environment.
- **Pause and reflect**: Take a moment to understand your discomfort—is it really one person who's causing you issues and you can avoid them? Are you projecting past pain onto a new group of people? Is it the norms themselves that you object to, or is it that you don't understand the norms? Understanding the norms in your environment better may help them bother you less or help you work around them.
- **Have a conversation**: When you're unsure or things aren't going well, ask. Often an open matter-of-fact conversation is all the fix that's needed. *What did you mean by . . . ?*
- **Find a comfortable balance**: No organization is a 'Borg' of mindless drones (if yours is, run away . . . fast!). Everyone is compromising a little, so you too can decide which norms you're good with and which you're OK to deviate from.

- **Don't buy-in to the myth of perfection**: You don't have to impress everyone, and no one is perfect, so give yourself and others a break. Set some reasonable boundaries you're clear with others about, and be willing to learn or adapt as needed.
- **Be open to feedback**: Feedback usually tells you just as much about the person giving it as your own actions. That's a good thing. So proactively reach out to people you admire and ask them for feedback—both positive and constructive so they can help you learn more about different ways to succeed in the context of your work environment. And if someone who doesn't want to help you gives you feedback, feel free to take it as permission to avoid them. More about giving and getting feedback in chapter 9.
- **Don't lose your sense of humor**: This is a sure sign you're overthinking how well you fit in or are showing up as being serious about everything (or the flipside—thinking everything's a joke).

Pro Tip: Learn the "rules" or norms of your environment first. Then you can figure out which rules you can break and when.

Women and people of color are told to play by the rules to succeed. But it's knowing what the rules are and then breaking some of them that is necessary to succeed and get more of what you want.

Good news! You've already got a head start on this by knowing your worth and priorities and how to negotiate or tradeoff to get more of what you want from section one. Well done!

Core People Skills

OK. Let's dive into the core people skills that will boost your career and confidence no matter where you work. How do you make others feel valuable? Thankfully it's not that hard. Here's a Top 10 list that will take you far:

1. **Listen**: This is Barack Obama's number one piece of career advice and I agree; and listening is even better when it's active—meaning asking questions, seeking clarity, repeating what you heard to help you and the other person connect and understand better.
2. **Remember names**: This is often a make or break for people (and admittedly one of my weak points; it takes work!) - use funny associations or alliteration if it helps; extra points for taking time to get to know them a little and remembering a fun fact as well.
3. **Communicate clearly**: Take time to organize your thoughts before hitting send on that chat message or email. Ask yourself: *Who needs to know/do what and why?* Keep it short and simple.
4. **Show up on time**: Some people think that showing up late to every meeting makes them seem important—Not. So. Much.
5. **Cameras on**: When you hop on Zoom, throw on a shimmer top or blazer over your PJs, or pick a calming image on your screen near your camera to focus on when it's hard to stare other people in the eyes, but "show up." The same is true for in-person gatherings. Showing up and meeting people face-to-face and in informal spaces builds trust. Large or small groups, 1:1, you decide.

6. **Give credit where credit is due**: Recognize and thank others—but avoid empty praise as you can usually find some positive truth to highlight. Like: *Your proposal was really well organized. That made it easier to think about the options.*
7. **Ask insightful questions**: And you'll look interested, engaged, and smart . . . and hopefully learn something useful for yourself. Like: *Tell me more about why you think X is better?*
8. **Don't pass blame and also don't apologize frequently**: Women especially apologize too often, so instead thank people for their patience/help/etc. or focus on what's been learned and how to improve. When you do need to apologize, acknowledge your impact vs. defending your intent.
9. **Ask if you don't know**: Need to know what the dress code norm is or how your senior director wants presentations done? Then just ask a helpful coworker.
10. **Don't complain**: OK, occasionally we all do it; don't make it a regular habit.

Pro Tip: There's an endless debate about women (especially women of color) showing up as "bossy" or "aggressive." Some say women shouldn't use "weak" feminine language. We've been told, *We're not bossy; we're the boss.* Others say women are expected by both men and women to be softer. Women are rewarded and more successful when they fit the stereotype.

It's all true. And it's not. I recommend ignoring any advice in this category. Instead, focus on what truly gives you confidence. If direct language and a focus on data is your natural mode of operation, then do that. If a softer language and reliance on EQ is your jam, then do that. You can be strong and empathetic and a good communicator in multiple styles. It's confidence that's the key.

Made it through this list without feeling the need for a Headspace meditation session? Great! Thinking a little mediation might be in order? No problem. People are complicated.

Ready for some people upskilling? **Revisit Section 2 of your personal career map: Setting Personal Goals to Create More Value for Yourself**. Keep it simple. Pick one to two items from the people-skills list above that will make your three- to six-month goal plan work better and add that in.

When you learn a new people skill well enough that it becomes habit, it takes less effort and frees your mind up for other things.

[Extra] Recommended Resources: *Latinas in Corporate: Overcoming Cultural Obstacles While Juggling a Career and a Family* by Myriam Del Angel OR *The Memo* by Minda Harts

Section Three

Avoid Common Work Problems

TLDR—Ever feel like your work life has plot twists and drama like your fave reality show? Yeah, this happens to the best of us. From bad bosses to surprise performance reviews and career limiting moves, this chapter tackles the most common problems employees face. We'll get context on why these issues are so common so you can dodge them like a pro. Made a mistake? No worries. You'll get tips on how to recover. Let's turn those plot twists into opportunities for career growth!

Reminder: The number one problem is not knowing your priorities (chapter 1). Once you use those to set your own goals, you'll have a lot more confidence in what you're getting out of work. That doesn't mean you won't run across problems or make mistakes, but it'll do a lot to minimize the biggest problem of feeling burned out, bored, underpaid, or just hating Monday mornings with a passion.

I've faced a lot of problems and made a lot of mistakes throughout my career. A lot. Some of them were highly regrettable. Many turned out to be a source of gratitude—because learning from these problems helped me move in a new direction that ended up being better for me.

Problems will happen. And everyone makes mistakes. If they tell you they don't, well . . . that's a mistake right there—lying. There's enough anxiety in this world; don't let your anxiety run away with you over how to handle common work problems. Made a mistake? No worries. The good news is you can recover from most mistakes. The recipe for recovery is simple, if not always easy:

- **Let go of your emotions**: Give your mistake a little space, and then put it in perspective—on a scale of 0-10, how big of a problem is it really?
- **Acknowledge the problem**: Tell your manager and anyone directly involved the facts of the situation, but no need to broadcast it to the world.
- **Show your readiness to fix it**: Offer a solution to the problem your mistake created or talk about what you learned that will stop you from making the mistake again.
- **Ask for guidance**: People are usually flattered by being asked their opinion or advice, and this can help them feel part of the solution with you.
- **Celebrate your recovery wins**: Not saying you should brag about making the mistake itself, but you can circle around later to remind your manager and yourself that you fixed it or learned something valuable that's made you better.

Repeated mistakes are important signals too. One mistake is . . . whatever. Make the mistake twice and it's worth considering what's going on. Three times and you have a pattern—which means you should take some action to change a habit, update your skills, or create an alternative way to address that issue. Pay attention to the signals, and you have the power to turn mistakes into something valuable. Every experience—good or bad—can be useful.

Well done, you! Recovering from a mistake is powerful. It gives you confidence and sometimes new skills. It can even make for a good example story in an interview. This is how you turn a mistake into a win.

There are times, unfortunately, when not handling a problem well (mistake or no) results in long-term damage. Some problems can mushroom, creating so much bad feeling that you and others around you are miserable at work. Some can cause you to lose focus and limit your ability to create value for yourself or others. Some can even get you blacklisted (when your negative reputation prevents you from getting new opportunities with your current employer or a new job elsewhere). If recovery isn't looking like an option, then making a good exit should be your focus (see chapter 10).

Insider Truth: While an employer can fire you for a serious mistake or a series of mistakes, they often won't. It can be easier and less expensive for them to simply "encourage" you to leave. They might give you a poor performance review, assign you the most tedious work, lock you out of key meetings, stop giving you feedback (positive or otherwise), or any number of things to make you feel unvalued. It's called "quiet firing." All of this is likely to hit all your anxiety and negative emotion buttons.

If this is your situation, the best thing you can do, the action most in your control, is to plan your exit. Ideally you can take time to line up a new job (even if it's part-time or temporary) before hitting the eject button. Still, if your wellbeing is shredded, then simply leaving and then figuring out your next steps outside of that negative environment is OK too. Whatever you do, don't stay *and fight.* You'll make it harder to recover and waste a lot of your own energy. You'll increase your risk of creating a negative reputation that extends beyond your current job (a.k.a. burning bridges).

The best that can happen is to avoid problems altogether. But you especially want to avoid the kind of problems that can create long-term damage or make you miserable. To that end, I'm going to share the four most common challenges we face in the workplace. These are the kinds of challenges that escalate into mistakes that are hard to recover from. They are also the ones most likely to lead us to quitting our jobs and hating work. Avoid these common problems and ensure work gets you much more of what you want.

Chapter 7

Avoid Hating Your Manager

TLDR— A bad boss is one of the most common workplace problems. It's almost guaranteed to happen to you, if it hasn't already. In today's workplace the screws are tightening around middle management. This is a scene that's going to continue to be tough. Let's get ahead of the why and how with tips that will help you and your manager beat the odds!

Ask a friend, read the results of the latest workplace survey, go online to a Quora forum and you'll see that hating your manager is still one of the top reasons people quit their job—if not the number one reason. It's certainly been reason enough for me once or twice. So what gives? Why does it happen so often? Does some kind of brainwashing happen to people when they become managers? Why do we have so many fabulously awful terms to describe people managers: the frozen middle, toxic leadership, micromanagers, yes-men, etc.? If this is such a common problem, why can't we solve it?

Since this is likely the number one barrier to loving your work, let's get serious.

What's Wrong with Your Manager Anyway

Middle managers (let's leave senior executives aside for the moment) are notoriously poor managers. There are lots of reasons for this, and it's usually not personal to you. Let's get some context and understand why they do some of the *WTF?* things they do. Knowledge is power, my friends.

1. **They're learning too**: I read this the other day: *You didn't know when you were growing up that you were watching your parents grow up too.* Mind blown. It's similar with most managers. While they are managing their team, they are learning how to manage. They will make mistakes.
2. **Higher turnover rates**: The average tenure is dropping from five-plus years to between 2-3 years.[xvii] Unsurprisingly companies are investing less and less in people development (especially manager development). Here's the math: if it takes at least one year to train someone up on management skills who will then be available for less than two or so years, it's not worth it to most organizations. This becomes a vicious cycle. Poor investment in management training creates an environment with poor managers learning from each other . . . and well . . . you can see where that's going.
3. **Unrealistic expectations:** Management today is usually individual contributor work + management work = two jobs. It's lots of paperwork, dealing with bureaucracy (a.k.a. herding cats), extra meeting time, more scrutiny, etc. on top of regular job responsibilities. Managers are often busier and under more pressure than you think.
4. **Emphasis on managing up**: Many managers are promoted for two reasons: high performer + they are good at managing

up (*not* because they already have great management skills for managing down; this they are expected to have the capability to learn, often on their own).

5. **Preconceived notions**: You were hired to solve a problem your manager doesn't have time, skills, depth of experience, patience, etc. to solve. You're there to eliminate that problem for them. That problem generally existed before you came on the scene. It's not about you.
6. **They're ambitious too**: Managers have their own goals (promotion, money, experience, kingdom building, etc.). Judging them for their ambitions won't change their minds.

Better understanding what's going on with your manager (and even their manager) makes things easier. Their jam may not be your jam, but at least you'll know what to expect. Confusion and holding the wrong expectations are the biggest source of problems between people and their managers. Avoid or fix this, and you're halfway there.

Managing Your Manager

Your manager can become your biggest champion. They can help you find resources, support your work-life balance, nominate you for new opportunities, and generally make your workday more gratifying. To get all this and more from them, you've got to give a little too. Let's take the list above and turn those challenges into solutions for making sure your manager trusts and empowers you:

1. **They're learning too**: Don't take their mistakes personally. Don't try to prove how much smarter you are. Give them some benefit of the doubt and be clear in your

communication with them to avoid confusion or bad assumptions.

2. **Higher turnover rates**: Give your manager the gift of feedback. Tell them when they do something helpful. Share suggestions on what might help your team work together better. And if you have constructive feedback for them, make sure you tell them why adapting their behavior will make it easier for you and others to solve the problems they care about.
3. **Unrealistic expectations**: If you have an opportunity to make their job easier, do it! For example: take meeting notes, track your own goals and projects well and on time, etc. I'm not saying buy and deliver their lunch for them. This is not about kissing up. It's managing up. Remember thinking about your own priority tradeoffs—time, money, or quality (chapter 1)? Find out what their top two priorities are and focus there.
4. **Emphasis on managing up**: Speaking of managing up, this is a needed part of making all organizations work, so lean in. Don't complain about your manager to their manager (they are predisposed to support the person they know better than you and who they hired or rely on to solve a particular problem). Instead, pay attention to how your manager makes decisions (where/who they want input from, what kind of data points help them feel confident), and lean into those preferences to get things done. Or just ask. Many managers will be happy you did. If you're managing up as much as you're managing down and across (peers, partners, more junior teammates), then you're doing it right.
5. **Preconceived notions**: Don't create or raise up new problems—not at least until you've solved the key ones your manager cares about. When they ask you to do something,

say: *I've got this.* You can always ask follow up questions or suggest alternatives next or make them aware of needed tradeoffs (example: *I can do this, but then my other project might be a week late. Is that OK with you?*). Give them the confidence you're capable and happy to do the work you were hired to do.

6. **They're ambitious too**: Support your manager's goals as they make sense to you. But also make sure your board of advisors knows what you're accomplishing. That way you're not putting all your eggs into one person's basket.

If you've built up trust with your manager, then you're much more likely to have the benefit of the doubt when a problem does come up (and they always do somehow). You'll also get more enthusiastic support when you share your own personal goals with your manager. More trust. More support. More choices. More success. This is what I want for you. Take time to invest in your manager so that it's easy for them to want this too!

When to Document

Having things in writing is your friend. If you are having problems with your manager (or someone else at work), and it's complicated or not getting fixed, then document your interactions. Detailed notes can do a few things for you:

1. **Help you reflect** on what your manager is trying to say or accomplish. Sometimes in the heat of the moment we mishear/misjudge what's really going on. Allow yourself that space and grace to reassess the problem from a distance.

2. **Help you better organize your approach** for the next conversation. Some possible options for changing up your approach and getting more specific documentation notes:
    a) Ask before attacking/accusing/etc. (Example: *What are you trying to accomplish? What's the main problem from your point of view? What would good look like?*)
    b) Ask them if they're willing to hit "reset" with you. (Example: *We've gotten stuck, and I'm having a hard time moving forward on this. Could we start over, take a fresh look? Would you be willing to tell me—again—what you'd like me to accomplish and how you recommend it gets done?* OR *I realize I never asked you what your style is, work preferences, pet peeves are. I'd love to start there again. I think it'd help me better get you what you need.*)
    c) Drive for clarity. (Example: *I heard you say I didn't deliver well on this project. I'm confused by this because I delivered the key items agreed on by the deadline set by the project team. Where is the gap that you're seeing?*)
3. **Serve as a set of documented facts** (when, what, who) if you do end up in a resolution conversation with the HR or People Team. If you weren't able to resolve the problem directly with your manager, you'll need this as a reference to help make your case.

Pro Tip: In several states you can't record a meeting via video or audio without notifying the other participant(s) and getting permission, but you can take notes when documenting. Make sure you write down what is actually said. Paraphrasing is interpretation and can derail your efforts. Even better if you're documenting in a shared doc so there's no confusion or changing of stories about what's been said and done.

The reality is that because the manager likely already has a track record of success, both as a performer and as someone trusted with managing the work of others, employers are biased toward supporting the manager in a disagreement. It's also very likely the manager already has more documentation on hand than you do because documentation is a part of their job as a manager. Hey, remember when your parents told you *life's not fair* after your sibling ate the last piece of cake? Yep, that rule still applies. If you approach a problem with your manager out of curiosity, show good intent, AND document your experience, you are much more likely to tip the scales of justice and get a positive outcome.

The goal here (as always) is to give you more tools, more choices. If you don't document what's going on (but rely on *he said, she said, they said*), then you risk not fully understanding what's going on, making a weak showing, and limiting your options for getting a better resolution.

[Extra] Recommended Resource: *Ask a Manager* by Alison Green

Chapter 8

Avoid Career-Limiting Moves

TLDR—It's what they don't tell you that gets you into trouble. Many of the rules of the workplace are never shared out loud. Many employees make career-limiting moves without even realizing it. This chapter will help you unlock the insider truths you need to know to avoid a career dead-end, tap into business IQ, and navigate confusing phrases like "bring your whole self to work." Plus you'll learn how to advocate for yourself. Crack the code and take control of your career!

If you want to avoid making Taylor's Swift's "Anti-Hero" your new personal theme song, then this chapter is for you. A breakdown with your manager might be the number one problem that limits your happiness and success, but this chapter is about the number two path to problems. This is a group of challenges that those in the business (HR, legal, leadership teams, etc.) call "career-limiting moves" or CLMs. These are the actions many people take without even knowing they are career-limiting. These actions can lead to getting fired outright, quiet firing or quiet cutting (making your work life so miserable that you quit), blacklisted (yes, it exists!), burnt bridges (destroyed relationships and reputation), being written up by your manager or HR, being involved in an investigation (for violating company policy), added to the list for the next layoff, and other sad outcomes. These things limit not only your ability to succeed in your current job; they can definitely limit you from future dream jobs. Avoid at all costs!

Top Examples of Career-Limiting Moves

What to avoid? Here's a list of the top ten career-limiting moves called out by insiders from a variety of industries:

1. **Shady behavior:** Gossiping, frequent complaining, or letting pressure negatively impact your performance and behavior
2. **Inability to take constructive feedback:** Not being open to feedback can hinder personal and professional development
3. **Lack of adaptability:** Resisting change, failing to adopt new technology, and refusing to learn new skills
4. **Poor communication skills:** Inability to effectively communicate ideas and collaborate with others
5. **Ignoring company culture**: Fighting the established culture can create conflict and confusion (Note: keep reading this chapter for tips on advocating for yourself and a cause without making a CLM)
6. **Lack of follow up:** Missing deadlines, being disorganized, waiting for others to tell you what to do, and agreeing to work without making effort
7. **Micromanagement**: Being overly controlling hurts team morale and productivity
8. **Non-inclusive behavior:** Disregarding the value of others, making offensive jokes, taking credit for others' work, and calling people names or making categorical assumptions

based on their race, gender, sexual orientation, or another identity group

9. **Failure to set boundaries:** Not knowing when to say no leading to burnout, a lack of work-life balance, poor performance, and is generally not a good feel or look
10. **Unethical behavior:** Engaging in dishonest or unethical practices, sharing private or sensitive information, or going against organization policy

Notice most of these examples are not about the numbers or job performance metrics? This is not about problems with hard skills. Career-limiting moves are almost always about people problems. Remember chapter 6 on seeing the value in others? That's a great place to go back and practice if you want to strengthen your game.

Almost all of these types of career-limiting moves are also too easily and quickly amplified in company social forums. A complaint that might have caused issues with your manager and team can now also raise flags for the head of people or HR and other leaders when it's posted to a broad company forum (like an all-employee chat group on Slack).

Pro Tip: If you wouldn't discuss it with people face-to-face, don't post it in an online channel.

What am I talking about here?

A complex but common example: Working caregivers, especially moms, struggled (are struggling) with return to office policies in the post-pandemic world. For some people this issue hits their panic buttons. Not surprising. This has been a tough change, and often one not well managed.

Lauren was one of those people. She had so much anxiety about an announcement requiring those local to a physical office to commute in for multiple days a week that she decided to post a detailed complaint and call-to-action (a boycott of the policy) in a broad company channel that included all employees (thousands of people).

Her post included personal protected health information (PHI details about her family's medical health that is protected under the law), personally identifiable information (PII details like where she lived and her doctor's name, practice, and advice that is meant to be protected by privacy laws), and details about exchanges with her manager that cast that person in a negative light. She included misinformation about how medical accommodations work and what the company's policy was in terms of manager discretion. Her story drove a lot of very understandable empathy, but it also exposed sensitive information about her doctor and family and spread confusion about the resources actually available to her fellow employees.

While Lauren's particular case was quickly solved with more flexible options for her to take care of her well-being and that of her family, she had created some other bigger problems. Her post had to be removed to protect PHI and PII and a new campaign to correct the misinformation she shared had to be distributed to solve for the confusion that followed. Worst, she lost trust with her manager and leaders of the company.

We are so used to posting about personal causes and issues on social media where almost anyone can engage however they choose in the moment, we sometimes forget how easily facts, nuance, and respect can get lost in social forums.

Insider Truth: Lots of workplaces now use an internal messaging app—like Slack, Teams, Google Chat, etc. While these tools were originally created for team-level collaboration, they often get used for broad company-wide communications too. They end up acting a lot like public social media forums (e.g., Instagram, WhatsApp, etc.). They've also brought some of the same challenges those platforms face but inside organizations. Polarization, trolling, cyber bullying, addiction to checking feeds, and likes validation (FOMO), etc.—it's all showing up in the workplace.

Unfortunately many organizations and leaders are inexperienced or hesitant when it comes to setting forum guardrails and rules of engagement. When these are not set up, a vocal minority of people can often take over broad forums, drowning out the voices of many of their fellow employees and shifting company culture. Being thoughtful about how you show up in online forums inside your organization is important. While your organization's leadership may not have explicitly shared rules of engagement, they often take action *after* an issue comes up, to the detriment of employees involved.

The Value of Business IQ

There's an inherent tension in the workplace. On the one hand, organizations, even nonprofit organizations, are driven by the need to bring in money. On the other hand, workers want to make money, advance their skills and careers, and to have a great environment to work in. This is all an expense for organizations. But most organizations are savvy enough to understand engaged, skilled workers offer a great return on investment. They know they are successful when you help them bring in more money than they spend on you. They don't exist to create your dream job. You own that dream. But they do better when they offer the conditions to help you make work worthwhile.

Ever since Millennials came onto the workplace scene, employers have been falling all over themselves to sell a mission- or purpose-driven culture, hoping to appeal to new generations of workers. Unfortunately this often ends up being overpromised and under-delivered. It can feel a lot like catfishing from the dating world (people pretending to be someone they're not). That's a big reason why the majority of workers today are feeling burnt out and turned off, seeing their jobs as mostly transactional. Organizational loyalty is at all-time lows. It's not so much that organizations are lying about a stronger focus on social causes and purpose-driven strategies (well, some are!) but mostly that it will never be the number one priority. We've done a great job of elevating more consciousness in business around lots of issues—equity, the environment, workers' rights, etc. We should keep working on all of this. AND at the end of day, we need to keep our work context in mind: business is business.

So the second thing to know that will help you avoid most career-limiting moves is having a strong foundation in business IQ or acumen. This may all seem obvious, but stay with me.

Businesses exist to solve problems. And if it were easy, then the organization would have too many competitors to make enough money. Expect problems to be a part of your job. That's what you're there for—to solve problems! (And try not to create additional ones.) Organizations exist to solve problems for other people, companies/organizations, industries, and/or governments by offering goods, products or services.

In order to stay in business, a company needs to make money (profits) and keep costs (losses) down or below the money they bring in while offering that good, product, or service. Again, even nonprofits have to ensure they can bring in enough funding to cover expenses and stay ahead of upcoming needs. This is why you often hear people talk about profit and loss balance sheets (P&Ls). This, my friends, is why companies exist. To bring more money in than they spend. Not to make your dream job come true.

Those are the business essentials everything else is based on. So you need to help your organization make money or save it. Or better yet, both!

Doing that? Great! Now you need to know how to explain how you're making the company money (or saving it). Section two offered a great way to make sure you understand your manager's goals, your own goals, and document them. Take a quick peek back and see if those goals reflect money earned or saved. If not, make an update to draw a more solid line between what you're doing and those dollar signs.

If you're not doing that (and well), then it'll be hard to argue the organization owes you more than you're currently getting (monetarily or non-monetarily) or that your ideas are better than others or that the organization should invest in your community, cause, or passion project—even if it's a great and needed idea.

Remember in the first section when we talked about different company environments (product, marketing, or service, operationally driven)? This will drive the company's approach and what part of business essentials they value most. Some examples:

- Product -> product innovation, streamlining development or manufacturing processes

- Marketing -> brand building, expanding revenue streams, creative ideas, etc.
- Service -> customer experience design, issue resolution, etc.
- Operational -> profit margins or risk reduction and savings

Knowing that can help you know how to focus your own efforts and shine (and determine if it's a great match for you).

You may be wondering why I took over 600 words to explain something so seemingly obvious. It's because not understanding (or in many cases forgetting or ignoring) this basic foundation of business has been the most common underlying cause of employee problems in the hundreds of cases I've seen during my career. No matter what they say, money comes first. We sometimes forget this bigger perspective in the heat of the moment (myself included).

(Maybe) Bring Your Whole Self to Work

Another way employers have tried to appeal to new generations, deal with the increased attention on social justice, and retain a greater diversity of workers is to pitch the idea that you can "bring your whole self to work." This is bull$hit. Many employers don't really want this. And really, the choice should be yours.

First, let's break it down. What do people mean when they say "bring your whole self to work" anyway? The motivation here is to give people space to be their authentic selves at work. To *not* feel they have to hide or cover parts of their identities, likes and dislikes, interests, or dreams and fears. Sounds reasonable. Sounds healthy. Sounds empowering, right? Yes! . . . and . . . before you share personal details about yourself, ask: *What does this mean to me?*

Does this mean sharing *everything* about yourself? Does this mean bringing *all* of your life into the workplace—your family dynamics, love life, medical history, politics, etc.? No. In fact, most organizations have policies (some in line with government policies like HIPAA protecting personal health information or PHI) to protect people's privacy, sensitive information, and well-being that set boundaries around these types of topics.

Beyond these types of policies, the boundaries of what your company culture will support may be pretty fuzzy. Some things to keep in mind: When you share your personal business with others, you are taking it out of the personal and placing it in the professional environment. Whatever you share will be taken into context with what's going on around you—office politics, competition among your coworkers, the readiness of others to understand parts of your lived experience that might be foreign to them, etc.

Yep, office politics are a fact of work life. Every organization has politics because organizations are groups of humans (and we misbehave), organized around hierarchical structures (creating competition), and driven by money. Power + groups of humans + money will produce politics every time. Coworkers who are your best friend one day can feel like your enemy the next. And often it's not because they are malicious or immature bastards (sometimes, yes). Usually it's because they are afraid—afraid of losing their job security, their opportunities, their reputation, their kid's health insurance, etc.

Here are a few other factors to consider. Some people are looking to make friends at work; others want to keep personal and professional separate. Some people may be introverts and less comfortable sharing personal details. Most people at work are interested in the *parts* of you that help them meet their work goals and make their work more fun, interesting, or easier. They are not as interested in your *whole* self. Does that make them disrespectful? Likely no. After all, we're all a bit selfish in nature and we only have so much capacity to take in information, social cues, and other people's experiences.

Insider Truth: Most organizations struggle with some real risks in supporting this concept of "bringing your whole self to work." Even DEIB leaders admit to struggling with talking about those risks in the workplace.[xviii] Here are some of the things that make this concept complicated in practice:

- The concept of "whole self" is at the same time broad and nuanced; it needs context to be fully appreciated.
- It doesn't give a lot of guidance for personal boundaries, which can vary greatly across a group of people.
- It requires everyone in the organization to support a safe space for a wide spectrum of realities.
- Boundaries of what's appropriate for professional settings vs. personal vary in different communities and cultures.
- Depending on the state you're in, different topics are not legally protected (e.g., LGBTQIA+ rights).
- While feeling that you can show up authentically contributes to mental health, well-being studies show that oversharing has shown the opposite effect—eroding work and life balance.

Looking for some more tips? Check out the **BetterUp** platform.

A mentor once warned me: "*No one at the office is your friend. Don't trust anyone.*" I was shocked. This was advice from an empathetic leader with a reputation for investing in a large diversity of people. As the years went on, I realized what they meant though. Don't trust anyone with your personal business. Don't trust anyone with your own success. You own both. And when push comes to shove, they will prioritize their own over yours. A good lesson. A hard lesson.

Researching new opportunities? Look for solid evidence of a healthy culture that embraces authenticity. Employers can help people be authentic and feel included at work. They can prioritize a diversity of representation. Even better, they can normalize ideas and practices that aren't the mainstream or majority held. They can also support a variety of communities that offer safe spaces and support for a diversity of people. This is what organizations can and should be doing—but aren't necessarily doing (well).

From here, I want this to be your choice. It doesn't need to be all or nothing. Be honest with yourself first about what you want to share in a work setting. Where your comfort level is. What beliefs or experiences are important to the work you're doing. Consider where your own threshold is for reflecting your beliefs vs. oversharing. Think about who you want to be vulnerable with. Maybe you want to step your way into it, first finding coworkers who also belong to your community so you have support. Maybe you've found a great business case for sharing more of your background and experience to design a better program or product.

Pro Tip: There's a great tool that's been used since at least Sun Tzu wrote *The Art of War*—situational awareness. It basically means the ability to observe, understand, and effectively respond to the situation unfolding around you. Using situational awareness, you decide what authentic strengths, concerns, interests, experiences, etc. to bring to the table. That could be to your job overall, to a particular project, or to a particular relationship or set of relationships.

Bringing your authentic self, your core essence to work—the aspects that make you *you*—is something we should all strive for—collectively. Regardless, make sure you're in the driver's seat when it comes to your own story.

Advocating Within the Workplace

None of this means you can't advocate for important issues or yourself within a workplace. Please do! The thing is to keep in mind that *how* you do it matters.

If your goal is to prove someone else or your organization is wrong or that your opinion is the only one that matters, then you'll struggle to succeed and the costs will be higher. Think Sophia in the beginning of the *GirlBoss* series who gets fired from retail after tearing into her boss for the umpteenth time. If your goal is to create change for the better, and you're willing to work with someone else or your organization to make that change happen, then you have a much better chance of success with your positive reputation intact. Like my therapist has repeatedly asked me: *Do you want to be right, or do you want to be happy?*

Context, timing, choosing the best forums, understanding the tradeoffs, understanding the communities you work within—all of these are important things to think about when advocating for an issue you care about. Like most things in life, a little balance in our approach goes a long way.

Ready for some tips on advocacy done well? Here you go:

- **Collect the facts**: Gather data, info, current policy, the "why" your organization currently does what it does for promotions/pay, or action on the issue, what's comparable, etc.
- **Find like-minded supporters**: Make sure they are also focused on positive change or supporting you.
- **Be open**: Let your manager and other people key to your success know what you'd like to achieve. You'll avoid surprising them when you take action, and they might have great ideas about how to move forward. Leave room for compromise if that's currently the best option (one step at a time is still a step forward).
- **Don't neglect your core work**: Meeting the requirements of your role and performing well will make it easier to promote your issue on top of that solid work performance.
- **Create space for discussion**: Bring people together to discuss current state and possible solutions. Make sure people know this discussion is about finding solutions rather than simply venting. Or if you're advocating for yourself (salary, promo, work-life balance), then set up a specific 1:1 with your manager so they know what you want to discuss.
- **Identify an executive sponsor**: If possible, bring a leader along on your journey to advise, guide, and amplify work toward a better solution or reinforce your case for promotion.

- **Know that timing matters**: Everything has a time and place; be aware of the context (around your work and/or the issue you're raising) that may (or may not) make it the best time.

I'll share a story about advocacy that's similar to examples I've seen pop up in multiple workplaces.

Advocacy example: Alex had been working in a highly competitive sales role for over a year when they noticed a trend. Despite the company's push to bring in more people of color for early career roles, by mid-career the mix was looking decidedly less Black and Brown, much more white and Asian. Alex, a member of the Black community themself, did some digging and found that many people of color left within the first year after a bad performance review or quit in frustration. Alex had seen this themself—friends and coworkers frustrated and leaving. Alex gathered some people together—a DEIB partner, Black and Latino community leads, a senior sales manager, etc.—to learn more about the problem. How could they help people of color be more successful and not waste those recruiting and onboarding dollars?

After a couple of months of investigation, Alex and the group had a data set and a proposed solution. They lined up a pitch session with the head of sales after quarter end, knowing the last quarter's numbers were great and their leader would be in a good mood—and maybe willing to spend on a new program. Alex helped write up the pitch but let two more senior and high-performing members of the Black and Latino communities present. This gave visible proof that people of color could be and were successful in these sales roles. They were also people who met with the head of sales regularly and knew that leader's personality.

The pitch was for a dedicated onboarding path run in partnership with the DEIB team. The data showed new people of color coming into the sales team were missing some of the cultural norms, business speak, and confidence many others took for granted. They were also much more likely to encounter racist remarks and *"I'd like to talk to your manager"* types of objections from customers. This onboarding path would give them a safe space to learn insider tips and get support. Managers would also get a quick onboarding supplement giving them context and tools for supporting new team members who might encounter these types of problems.

The pitch was clear about the cost of recruiting and onboarding early career talent and how much smaller the onboarding path spending would be. They showed the return on investment (ROI) potential was almost two times what the current early career cohort was making in sales, if they were better supported. "*You just had a great quarter. Imagine if we doubled that in one year,*" they asked the head of sales.

Break out the bubbly. The head of sales was impressed. The group was given funding and two quarters to test it out and report back. In the next cycle's performance review (six months later), Alex cited their role in the program and the ROI on top of doing great work in their sales role. It helped seal the deal on their promotion. Love it!!!

It's a fabulous feeling to know you've made your corner of the world better! Giving yourself a better chance of success is even more fabulicious. If you know how to negotiate with others in the context of a business environment, then you've got the tools, truth about workplaces, and tips to get more of what you want. You can avoid career-limiting moves AND be a better advocate for yourself and others. This is, my friends, a WIN, WIN, WIN!

Tools: Personal Career Map |Avoid Common Work Problems (Avoid Career Limiting Moves—10 min.): Free download here: www.jomcrell.com/free

Pull out your personal career map, take a five-minute meditation break, and then let's get some focus on the things you want to avoid.

For this exercise, we're going to break it down in three quick steps.

Step 1: First, you're going to choose one to two things you want to avoid at work. This could be something you're already having problems with, something you've had problems with in the past, or something you could see becoming a problem. To keep it simple and doable, only pick one to two at a time. When you've nailed those, you can always add something to the list.

Done that? Excellent!

Step 2: Here you can go back to the fix-it list at the beginning of section three and choose the one to two fix-it actions you can apply. Have some additional notes or another approach? Awesome. Just don't overcomplicate it.

Finally, **Step 3:** Let's put that in action by choosing a place and time for putting that fix-it into action. When you've got a plan AND you've thought ahead to when and where you can use that plan, you're making it very likely you'll make good things happen!

Chapter 9

Avoid a Bad Performance Review

TLDR— Do performance reviews get your heart beating fast? And not in an "I love you" kind of way? This doesn't have to be the case. Performance reviews should and can be *no surprise* moments. Let's break down how performance reviews work, what you need to prep like a pro, how to handle feedback, and get the growth and recognition you deserve!

There are, unfortunately, several things that can lead to a bad performance review—different expectations from your manager, lying about your accomplishments, pissing people off while accomplishing your goals, not meeting your goals, biases, etc.

What's the worst mistake? Not documenting your accomplishments well. What, you say?!? My performance speaks for itself! OR I've done a great job of hiding my poor performance (Yikes!). Either way, you've proven nothing by not documenting your work except that you're not very organized and/or don't value the performance-review process. Not a good move because this is typically a pain-in-the-a$$ process for your manager that you've now just made harder.

Setting Yourself Up For a Great Review

Sooooo, make this easier on yourself. Set up a performance file. Be optimistic. You can call it "[My Name's] Rocket-to-the-Moon Performance File." Whatever you call it—use it! Now. Today.

Start documenting what you've agreed to accomplish with your manager as well as your goals, checklist or milestones, and accomplishments from the start of your project (or six-month review cycle). Try to be as specific as possible. For example:

- **Core Work**: Top three to five work projects you've agreed to with your manager (see chapter 4)
- **Personal goals**: Your three- to six-month goal plan (see chapter 5). Reminder: Get specific. Make it timebound. Share your goals.
    - Goals should be defined by results. Don't write: *Improve process XYZ.* Not good enough. Try: *Introduce a new (cheaper, better) tool to make XYZ process faster/better, and then update the documentation for XYZ process to make it easier for other people to use the improved process.*
    - Goals should be broken down into bite-sized chunks with deadlines to help you manage your time and check-in with your manager's expectations. Example here:
        - (June) Research new or better tools
        - (1st half of July) Socialize tool options including pros and cons and my recommendation on best tool choice for this company/team with process stakeholders—my manager first

        - (2nd half of July) Create a plan and implement the new tool
        - (August) Document and train others on the new tool as needed
        - Congrats! Process improved for many employees. Money saved or made (quantified as you can). Great work!
- **Thank yous:** Someone sent you a thank-you note? Post kudos on Slack or Teams? Save it in your review file.
    - Were they specific about why they love you? Good. If not, say thanks, and then ask what specifically made them happy. File that too.

Check in with your manager once a month and make sure your goals and milestones are in line with what they expect. Be specific. Ask: *What have I been doing well? What could I be doing better? What does an "Exceeds" vs. a "Meets Expectations" performance for my role look like?* Take notes. File it.

When it's time for the formal performance review process, use your notes to summarize what you accomplished and how you did it so well. It'll take less time AND you'll have the proof for a great review rating in your well-documented file.

How Performance Review Cycles Work

Looking to not only meet expectations but exceed them? Good. I like your energy! Understanding the behind-the-scenes process for performance reviews can help. Here are the key components:

- **Self-Reviews**: This is the part of the process where you have to summarize what you did during the review period and make a case for a good rating and/or promotion. Again, if you've been documenting your manager's goals, your goals, etc., then you're set.

- Just focus on results and don't include all the details of the project to keep it short, sweet, and effective.

- **Peer and Manager Reviews:** Often your manager needs to write their own summary of your performance. You may need to collect feedback from 3-5 peers, so be thinking ahead about who can provide positive feedback and speak to the skills you most want to highlight.
  - **Your manager:** Again, if you've been documenting goals with your manager and they have access (Example: in your 1:1 meeting document), you've made their life easier because they can copy/paste. AND they are more likely to have a positive view of what you've accomplished. They'll turn this in with a suggested rating and promo nomination (if that's relevant).
  - **Peers:** You can help your peers (and yourself) out by giving a starting summary with your request for performance feedback that focuses on the things you want to highlight. Example: *We worked together on XYZ project when my role was to help the team align on strategic decisions, delegate all design work, and deliver our updated brand story. Can you share what I did that was the biggest win for the project and what I could take away to make future projects even better?*
- **Ratings**: Ratings are reviewed and adjusted to fall into a bell curve across the entire organization, with most people getting a middle rating (~60%) and small numbers of people getting

poor (~15%) and very poor (~5%) or excellent (~15%) and super excellent (~5%) ratings on either side.

- Most organizations won't give you a rating above the middle for your first six months to first year (as you're supposed to be learning the role and organization).
- A poor rating usually leads to a formal performance improvement plan (PIP) for a three- to six-month period and is essentially like being on probation.
- A middle rating (like meets expectations) is NOT a bad rating. If you act upset or discouraged by a middle rating, you may annoy your manager. Instead, try: *This is a great review. I'm ready to take this feedback and accelerate from here. What would an exceeds rating performance look like for the next review period?*

- **Calibrations**: This process involves managers and/or leaders reviewing the distribution of ratings and promotion across teams. Your performance never stands on its own; it's in the context of a comparison across all similar roles in that review period.
    - During calibrations leaders are mostly looking for outliers (poor or excellent ratings or promotion nominations). This is an opportunity to compare expectations for similar roles and levels and should also be a time when they specifically review for bias.
    - If no one has a similar role to you, you may have a hard time rising above a middle rating or getting a promotion. Since calibrations are a comparison exercise, you'll need to work with your manager on

building a strong business case for your unique role and progress.

- If you don't market yourself beyond your manager and team, it'll be harder for your manager to compare you favorably (and above) others. Remember, all managers are advocating for their team members in this exercise (or giving the rationale for a poor rating). To stand out, having another advocate from your board of advisors can help!

- **Promotion Nominations**: Most organizations use a promotion standard that requires proof of performance at the level you want to be promoted to for at least three to six months.
    - That means they expect you to show you can do the job you'd like to be promoted to *before* you get paid for it. This could be more than three to six months as you move higher and roles become more complex. Taking on stretch projects that show delegation, good decision-making, providing more than one solution with tradeoffs considered, etc. are all good ways to "show" you're performing at your desired promo level.
- **Compensation Discussion**: Some organizations split the performance review and compensation discussion, but most organizations have a performance-based aspect of compensation (bonus or commission or similar). Sometimes compensation is reviewed and adjusted with each performance cycle, sometimes just once a year. Since it depends on each organization and their fiscal year calendar, take some time to look it up and understand what to expect.

Looking for tips on negotiating a promotion or raise? Check out the tips in chapter 2.

Insider Truth: If you are rated with poor performance and put on a performance improvement plan (PIP), your best option is usually to move to a new organization. If you want to keep your job, take it seriously, act enthusiastic about doing better, and be specific with your manager about what improvement and a meets rating would look like.

However, know a PIP will stay on your record even if you recover or move to a new role within the organization and will make managers wary of your skills and performance. Many times managers will put you on a PIP hoping you leave. Often finding a new role that's a better match for your skills or environment needs is going to take less energy and get you better results.

Knowing what the parts of a performance review cycle are, what managers are considering, and what your performance will be compared to can definitely help you. Many companies are moving toward an "always on" performance management system (prioritizing regular check-ins over annual reviews). Some small companies may not have a well-documented or formal performance review process. Regardless, checking in with your manager on your goals and progress on a regular basis, making the process easier for your manager (with good documentation), and curating an advocate or two in leadership in addition to your manager can go a long way to a successful performance management outcome!

Avoiding Bias in Reviews

There are all kinds of biases that happen during employee processes like performance reviews. Bias is an ingrained tool our human brains use to remember more stuff, make quick judgments or decisions, and shortcut our way to getting more done. You can easily balance against some bias (example—recency bias). Some, unfortunately, you may not be able to (example—racial or gender bias). HR or your People Team and leaders can and should put in place training and checkpoints to reduce bias in processes like performance management. But know that bias will happen.

Disclaimer: If you're experiencing harassment or discrimination, report it! Don't suffer in silence. Worried about retaliation, not being taken seriously, or finding the situation uncomfortable? Many organizations offer an anonymous channel to report concerns. Regardless, there is usually more than one way to report it—your manager, your manager's manager, someone in HR, a tool (example—a hotline or online form), etc. Or move to a new job (if you can).

Here are some common biases. Being aware of these can help you counter and avoid them:

- **Recency Bias:** Focusing on recent events or achievements rather than considering the entire performance period. Impact: ignores long-term contributions and weights recent activities too much.
- **Halo Effect:** Allowing one positive aspect of an individual's performance to overshadow the value of other areas. (The opposite can also be true.) Impact: skewing the overall review based on a single characteristic.

- **Negativity Bias:** Giving more weight to negative information or experiences rather than considering positive aspects. Impact: overemphasizes shortcomings and can be unfairly critical.
- **Confirmation Bias:** Giving more weight to information that confirms preexisting beliefs or expectations about an employee. Impact: ignores contradictory evidence and can lead to an inaccurate review.
- **Race, Gender or Similar Biases:** Evaluating individuals based on stereotypes rather than objective performance criteria. Impact: unfairly favoring or creating a disadvantage for employees based on stereotypes rather than merit.
- **Affinity Bias:** Preferring employees who share similar characteristics, backgrounds, or interests with the evaluator. Impact: overlooking diverse talents and perspectives, leading to a lack of inclusivity.
- **Attribution Bias:** Assigning success or failure to internal factors (personal traits) while neglecting external factors. Impact: blaming or crediting the individual for outcomes beyond their control.

Pro Tip: Counter bias by . . . you got it . . . documenting what you've done and how you've done it. It's hard to argue with hard facts. And have regular conversations with your manager about your performance each month (or at least once BEFORE the formal performance review cycle).

Giving Feedback

So it's performance review time, and you've got an inbox full of peer-review requests? Good on you for being popular! First rule: rarely, if ever, share negative feedback in a formal review cycle. Remember what our grandmothers told us? *If you don't have anything nice to say, don't say anything at all.* And, *You catch more flies with honey than vinegar.* Grandma may not know what TBH means and maybe she's never watched TikTok, but she knows what she's talking about here. Humans haven't changed too much. These sayings are still true. When you have positive feedback to share with someone, do it. Performance cycle or not, people will love this—so share anytime. They will remember working with you as a positive.

If you have truly constructive feedback (a.k.a. the goal is to improve things vs. rant), then share it. But *first* make sure you've shared the feedback directly before a formal performance review. Sharing feedback in the moment or shortly after gets the best results. And if you're sharing it again in a performance review (because it's unresolved), be thoughtful about how you do it. Make sure to share any positives first and word the constructive feedback in an authentic, but optimistic, can-be-improved way. For example:

- *JD is always willing to jump in and help troubleshoot problems on the team. There are times when the problem at hand is not serious and doesn't require the level of research and escalation that JD has provided. This can slow the project timeline. For example, . . .*
- *Veronica is an important member of our team as our software quality control manager. Her ability to find bugs quickly is key to keeping us on our project timeline. However, there are times when Veronica has not communicated or documented*

the bug. This can delay the team if they have to revisit the code and incorporate a fix. For example . . .

Now this doesn't mean lying or hiding a problem. It means focusing on the positive wherever possible and using that as a springboard to suggest a reasonable change. Let's try another example:

- First attempt: *Terry is always rude, hating on me and other people. I don't want to work with them anymore.*
  - This kind of feedback quickly becomes a useless blame game. Because Terry could say: *You're always complaining. It's hard to work with you.* Instead, stick to the facts; ask yourself what about Terry being rude is a problem? And be specific!
- Better Alternative: *Terry often sidetracks project conversations with comments like, "You won't get it done on time anyway." Or, "If you really knew what you were doing, you would have . . ." This kind of comment makes it hard to understand if there's really a specific problem we can or should solve, and if so, I'd love to hear Terry identify the problem earlier in the process and propose a solution.*

Looking for more help on how to give feedback? Well, there is no shortage of feedback frameworks out there. If you find one that is useful to you, or that your organization uses, go for it! Here are a few common framework options you can Google:

- **SBI** (Situation—Behavior—Impact)—a framework focused on helping you give feedback that is focused, specific, and objective
- **Radical Candor**—a framework and book by Kim Scott that focuses on creating feedback that is both kind and clear, specific, and sincere

- **Feedforward** (Reflect, Inquire, Suggest, Elevate)—a framework that focuses on solutions rather than mistakes, on the future rather than the past

Pro Tip: Regardless of how you frame your comments, always focus your feedback on the work (the what and how) versus the person (the who).

Getting Feedback

Feedback is a gift. Heard this one before? Trying not to gag on that oversized cliché? Yeah, me too.

That said, feedback is going to happen. Positive feedback is lovely. Seek it and enjoy it! But everyone gets hard feedback at some point. Even after years of not only getting feedback but writing advice and facilitating feedback training, I still feel my defensive walls go up when I first hear critical feedback. Sometimes I wanna give feedback about how the feedback was given—rude! But having a feedback meltdown is not helpful. It's hard on our wellbeing. So here are three top tips I've found that work really well for this:

1. **Give it space**—It's OK to not be OK when first receiving hard feedback.
    a) There's almost always an emotional impact—good or bad. To buy space, you can say something like: *I always appreciate getting feedback, especially if it helps me do better work. I'll read this in more depth and think about how I can apply it.* Noncommittal except that you'll digest it. You don't have to process it immediately. Recommend waiting 24 hours.

2. **Consider the source of feedback**—Feedback reflects as much about the people giving it as the person receiving it.
    a) Feedback is valuable insight. It tells you about the other person's priorities, their perspective on what good work looks like in their sphere of the world, and what pressures they are facing. If you can address those aspects or learn from them, it'll be a lot easier to reshape the conversation as needed in new or alternate directions that benefit what you're trying to accomplish.
    b) Example: *You've been slow to turn in your work lately.* This could translate to: *My manager values time to review and comment before team meetings.*
3. **Try to find something valuable about it**—Give that feedback the squint test after you've given it some space. You might find there's something there that's useful after all.
    a) In the previous chapter we talked about how many problems are rooted in people skills and the specific environment we're working in—*how* we do our work. This is often why feedback stings—it feels personal. Try to view the feedback as a comment on a skill set that can be learned or applied as needed in that environment—not personal commentary on your value as a human being or career potential overall.
    b) Is the feedback clear? If not, it's more than OK to ask for more info. Good questions to ask: *Can you share a specific example of when this applied? What do you think would have worked better? Was the main challenge what I did or how I did it?*

Insider Truth: People of color and women are less likely to get valuable feedback. Unfair, but true. It's often called "protective hesitation"—people being uncomfortable with giving feedback to someone who's different from them.

Feedback is critical to navigating your work environment, building stronger relationships, and getting more opportunities. Here are three ways you can get quality feedback:

- **Ask for it:** I shared this in chapter 6, but it's worth repeating: Proactively reach out to people you admire and ask them for feedback. Show that you're open to getting better.
- **Get specifics:** Make sure you're getting actionable, skills-based feedback. Prompt the person you're asking for specifics. Example—*I'm working on X skill. Do you think I'm improving?*
- **Counter bias:** It's OK to push back if the feedback you're getting is based on bias. Example—*You're too aggressive.* Counter: *Would you give the same feedback to a man on this project?*

Chapter 10

Avoid a Bad Exit

TLDR— Moving on? Make sure you take a great reputation with you, as well as plenty of support for your next move. Whether you are leaving a fab experience or the worst, this is all about owning your story, making a smooth transition, and getting the max out the value you built while in the role.

Gotta go? Sometimes, no matter what you do, your dream job is not going to happen in your existing environment. Or maybe you've just outgrown it. Whether you found you'd been dropped into your own personal version of *Mean Girls*, the work isn't what you signed up for, or you're just ready to move on to the next opportunity, whatever the reason—good or bad—DO NOT make a bad exit.

What's a bad exit? Anything that hurts your reputation. It's a small world after all—especially in the working world. The chances that you'll run into people you worked with again is pretty high. The chances that you'll run into someone who knows someone you worked with is even higher. This is why they call bad exits "burning bridges." And while you may have done great work while you were there and made some great relationships, if you leave on the negative, people will remember that just as much or even more than all those positive experiences you created.

Pro Tip: A good exit is worth more to your career than a great entrance.

So don't create drama on your way out. Don't be arrogant. Don't spread gossip or talk $hit, try to undermine a coworker who made your working life difficult, leave a project in a bad state, etc. It's tempting sometimes (Yes! More than tempting sometimes . . . been there), but focus on yourself and getting yourself to as positive and meaningful a place as possible. Leave the consequences for everyone else to karma. Let the universe take care of bad actors. It usually does (eventually). Aim to leave your team, manager, and organization with a smile on your face—even if it's killing you inside. Take the high road. That's your upper hand. Otherwise, they control the story of your exit.

I recommend doing three things to create a great exit for yourself—get exit recommendations, write a great exit note, and be (somewhat) honest in the exit survey.

Get Exit Recommendations

People typically give at least a two-week notice when they exit. It's a sign of respect to your employer, giving them time to plan for the transition, but it also gives you time to write your own exit story. The first thing you'll want to do is reach out for recommendations (if you haven't already curated some during your time in role). You can use recommendation statements on your LinkedIn profile, in a specific recommendation section on your résumé, and in examples during interviews. In some industries, employers may still be asking for a formal recommendation letter, so it's good to have these lined up in advance.

Insider Truth: Some employment policies or types of roles will lead to an immediate exit. If you are going to a competitor or have a conflict of interest, they may terminate your employment and take back access to equipment and files ASAP. Read up on your employee policy/handbook and be prepared.

Take advantage of the coworker connections you have direct access to. Ask 2-3 people—who you have a good relationship with or who you've helped recently—for a recommendation statement. Ideally, at least one of these is from your board of advisors (see chapter 5 on who these people can be), could also be any peer, a client or partner, and/or someone with a more senior position with something positive to say.

Always offer a draft making it clear they can edit however they like. Why? Two reasons: 1) then you can focus on the particular skills, experiences, attributes that you want highlighted, and 2) it shows the other person that you value their time and energy by not making them draft it from scratch.

What does a good recommendation statement look like? It focuses on specific skills—at least one hard and soft or people skill—and offers a brief example. It tells people what someone most liked about working with you. Did you help make or save money? Have them include that. Here's a generic example:

I loved working with [Name]. [She/They/He] made an immediate impact on our team. [Name] is [people skill like–quick to build rapport with clients]. Beyond that, [Name] is an impressive [hard skill expertise like–financial analyst] who is able to [result you helped them achieve]. Without [Name] we wouldn't have [results statement with money earned or saved].

Feel free to get creative with the wording, especially if you're in a more casual industry environment or trying to stand out on LinkedIn. Clichés like "team player" will not be as impressive as more original examples or descriptions. If you're looking for skills to highlight that might help you get your next dream job, look up some LinkedIn profiles of people doing that work and borrow some keywords that you can apply to your own work. Ask an AI tool you trust what its recommendation is.

Pro Tip: Worried that collecting endorsements will tip off someone that you're planning/want to leave? Just tell them you periodically update your profile, and this is part of it. They'll be so impressed with how proactive and organized you are!

Write a Great Exit Note

First thing's first, this is not the same thing as a resignation notice. Make sure to submit an official resignation letter. You'll need to email this to your manager and HR partner (or HR team)—ideally after talking it through with them live. It should include: your last date of employment, a brief thank you, short summary of next steps (including an offer to meet with your manager to create a transition plan), and be signed (electronically is usually OK). Have a conversation with your manager about how your exit will be communicated—who should know first, if your manager will send a note, and that you plan to send a personal exit note after.

Your exit note, on the other hand, is a way to own your story as you leave. It's essentially a farewell note to your coworkers. But it's also a way to manage how you want to be remembered. Here are some things to keep in mind when writing your exit note:

- **Don't send it to the entire company** (unless it's a small company and you truly worked with everyone at some point).
- **Send it to those you worked with directly** and everyone on your team (don't leave out someone on your direct team to markedly show your dislike).
- **Keep it short and sweet** (I'm talking three paragraphs or roughly 250 words max.).
- **Share 1-3 highlights** on what you learned from working there (note the focus on "learned" so as to avoid just sounding like you're just bragging)
- **Say thank you** (for the things you genuinely appreciated).
- **Always keep networking** by inviting folks to reach out via LinkedIn, email, or wherever you track professional connections (you can always ignore requests from anyone you don't truly appreciate).
- **Share where you're going next** (note: you don't have to if you don't want to or don't know—Example: *Stay tuned. I'll share more about what I'm doing next soon.*).

Recency bias is real. It will definitely hurt you if you leave a bad taste in everyone's mouths. It will definitely help you if you leave with a positive message that showcases you at your best. A good transition and a great exit note will go a long way to helping you leave on a high note.

If you were laid off (that sucks, sorry!) or were fired (ouch!), you can still write a (positive!) exit note—but it'll be a post on LinkedIn vs.

an email internal to your previous employer. Again, the main point here is to boost your reputation and leave a record of how you want to be remembered. You can use essentially the same points above for this type of post. It's OK to note that you were laid off, but it likely doesn't help to say you were fired.

Pro Tip: If you believe you were wronged when you were fired, you should get an employment law lawyer and seek legal advice, including what to share and what not to share with your (former) employer. An exit note or transition plan is not the time to rant about bad history. It's about you and your future.

Exit notes are a great way to gather those connections who are supportive and have a positive impression of you to rally and amplify your skills, experiences, and dreams for what's next. For your closest coworkers and partners, take a moment to make a personal connection (phone call, quick Zoom) to tell them thanks and share what's next. They'll love it and be ready to support you. You've got a great future! Go get it!

Exit Survey—TBH or Not TBH

When you leave voluntarily, most organizations will ask you to complete an online exit survey. Some may actually set up an exit interview with someone in HR. Since exit surveys are one channel of feedback that not only HR but many leaders pay some attention to, they are often worth your while to complete. However, you'll have to decide how honest you want to be. They are never completely anonymous (no matter what they say).

I recommend having someone specific in mind when you share. Think of someone you worked with who's in a neutral position—not your bestie coworker and not the person you hated having meetings with but just someone you worked with once. Imagine sharing your feedback with them. Keep it general—*looking for more career development opportunities, needed more flexibility, found more competitive pay, didn't feel management was supportive of my success, etc.* Naming someone specific in your exit survey from a negative view is not going to do much except make you look bitter, harsh, or petty. If you have specific ideas on improving that work environment, go ahead and suggest those.

Insider Truth: HR will roll up your exit survey or interview feedback into general categories. They're interested in trends more than an individual's experience. They'll slice and dice the data and see if there are hot pockets—teams with a concentration of exits or feedback themes. Thinking about and giving feedback in those terms makes your feedback more valuable.

Also, the exit survey is not the best way to raise concerns about policy violations, mistreatment, harassment, and discrimination. If you do include that in your exit survey (vs. a reporting channel before you leave), be aware that someone at the company may follow up (because again, exit surveys are never truly anonymous).

There are, of course, also places to leave feedback for organizations in the public sphere—example: Glassdoor. Same advice applies here. Leave the names aside and focus on categorical feedback that helps someone who doesn't know anything about you or your situation understand the pros and cons of that environment. If you use workplace review sites as a way to help others make their own informed decisions (vs. a personal explanation of your work history), then you've done them and yourself a favor.

Now it's time to move forward and focus on you and your future.

Section Four

Build for Your Future (In the Future of Work)

TLDR—Feeling like your workplace is stuck in the last century? You're not wrong. We're navigating the future of work—think flexibility and autonomy (no more 9-5), AI and upskilling (augmenting your intelligence), and debunking productivity myths (measuring your performance in new ways). Since organizations are struggling to adapt to all this change, you'll own more of your career success and development. Get ready to embrace your future!

Work is changing. Where work gets done, by who, with what skill sets and how work is structured—these are all evolving quickly in our post-pandemic world. This is what's commonly called the "future of work" by those trying to get ahead of fast-changing employment trends.

How did we get here and where are we going? A couple of very good questions. Questions I've heard often—during layoffs, all over LinkedIn posts, in senior leadership meetings, and as the basis of many a discussion in Quora forums. The cost of living today is out of whack with salaries. Talking about buying a house earns you a well-deserved eye roll from Gen Z. Debt from student loans keeps climbing. Caregiving costs are soaring. Burnout and work-life balance continue to top the charts in Google searches and AI bot chats. Commuting is super painful no matter how many great podcasts you listen to on the way. And, as of publishing this book, almost 90% of Fortune 500 companies are still run by men (with ~75% of the top 50 run by white men).

The Old Model of Work

Things are not feeling balanced. The post-WWII working model of traditional office life (think the *Mad Men* TV series) that got us to this point is not serving (most of) us well anymore. Hasn't been for a while. That old model for work was based on several things:

- **Single income households:** A "traditional family" structure with the husband working and the wife taking care of home and children[xix]
- **The rise of the professional class:** Mostly white men in this class with the focus on the physical office as the center of productivity and access to tools and teams
- **Distinct and physical workplaces:** 9-5 work culture and a reliance on physical workplaces created a separation between work and home priorities and stresses
- **Short commutes:** Daily average commute of roughly 30 minutes[xx]
- **Pedigree-based hiring:** Assessing the value of workers by college degrees, previous employer brands, certifications, having an MBA, or some other institutional stamp of approval vs. a direct evaluation of skills, experience, and potential

- **Productivity & performance metrics:** Tracking activity, presenteeism (butts-in-seats), and widgets created that favors a manufacturing environment
- **High tenure:** Boomers typically staying with their employer up to ten years with a strong sense of company loyalty[xxi]
- **Financial stability**: Over 60% of Americans in the middle class with strong buying power[xxii]

So many employees talk about feeling like a cog in the wheel. That's because the old model of work was built for a different time and optimized for the Industrial Revolution—a reality that doesn't exist anymore. Leaders are feeling this too. Productivity levels have continued to decrease since the 1970s—despite tech innovations like the internet.[xxiii]

The New Reality of Work

That is not our reality anymore. Today we're seeing a pretty wide gap from that model centered on traditional office life. Many of today's trends began back in the 1980s:

- **Multi-income households:** All adults in the household usually working outside the home in order to support a middle-class lifestyle[xxiv]
- **The rise of purpose-driven work:** Less trust in public institutions and government places; more pressure on companies to provide a sense of purpose and address social issues
- **Blended work-life balance:** Less of a distinct gap between professional and personal. Smartphones and technology have blurred the lines. Life is happening! And work is happening at the same time!

- **Longer commutes:** Commutes doubled to an average of one hour per day[xxv]
- **Skills-based hiring:** A focus on the evidence of skills (rather than credentials) matched against work needs expanding the diversity of qualified candidates and supporting more fluid careers[xxvi]
- **Productivity and performance metrics:** A shift toward outcomes or impact created, skills developed, and other measures of creative and strategic problem-solving
- **Shorter tenure:** Millennials and Gen Z tenure averages between 2-3 years and 12-plus job changes in a lifetime with a growing shift to career changes, not just job changes[xxvii]
- **More financial uncertainty**: A ~80% increase in wages not keeping up with the cost of living that has increased 300-400% since the 1970s.[xxviii] The BIG hitters: housing, medical care, caregiving, and (ouch! especially for the professional worker) student loans
- **New economic drivers:** The rise of the "sharing" (think Airbnb) and "creative" (think influencers on TikTok and YouTube) economies changing how value is created
- **New technology**: The advancement of technology makes asynchronous collaboration possible—no longer needing to be in the same place and timezone (like a traditional office) to be highly productive. AI creating tech disruption, driving what work machines vs. humans do and what productivity looks like

It shouldn't be surprising that the old model of work isn't working anymore in this new reality. And yet, it is surprising . . . to many organizations and leaders who are having a hard time adjusting. To be fair, many of those organizations and leaders got to their current-day success using that old model. It worked for them. It's hard to let go of something that made you successful. On top of that, most of these organizations have grown using processes, norms, tools, business models, etc. that are founded in that old model. It's hard to change quickly at scale.

I think of it as the difference between a cruise liner and a speedboat. The cruise liner has a LOT of amenities (hello, restaurants, fitness centers, organized activities, and more!), it supports a large ecosystem of many different people and roles, and it works on a predictable timetable and service-delivery model. But because of this, it takes a loooooong time to make a change and turn around. For many organizations piloting the cruise liner, this change is going to take a lot of coordination, investment, and maneuvering. If you're in a speedboat, you're more at the mercy of the socioeconomic waves and weather around you, and you've got to pack your own lunch, but you can make a quick turn any time you want. Either way, we're all feeling some #futureofwork wobbles.

This is why you'll own more of your own career development in the future. There's an advantage in that—more choice. And of course, there's also a challenge too—more responsibility, more self-advocacy. We're all going to need some tools, tips, and insider truth to navigate this change (and the ups and downs that come with it).

A New Definition of Success

Regardless, I'm seeing some promising signs along the way. The path to success, so narrowly defined in the old model of climbing the corporate ladder, has broadened. Forget the ladder or even the newer "jungle gym" analogy. When work success is no longer the destination but a toolbox to help you live life—the possibilities are much BIGGER. This more open vision allows so many more options for what success can look like, as well as more paths to get there.

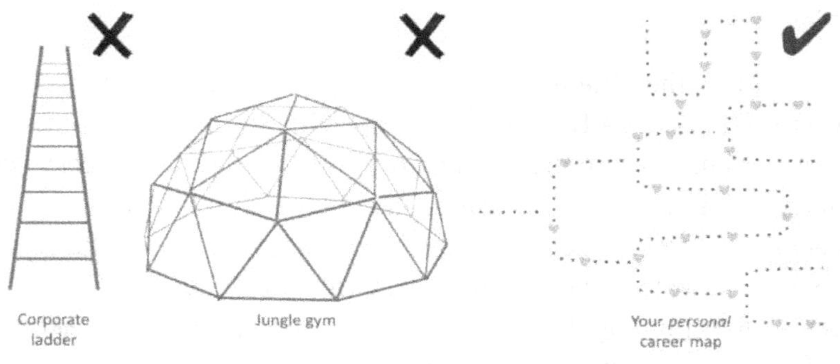

These new options for organizing work can also better fill skill gaps, bring organizations more agility, increase productivity, and more. They can help a greater diversity of people create value with more autonomy or control over their work. And there are lots of options. Some key examples: experimentation with flexible work arrangements, fractional work models, skills-based hiring, acceptance and support for more career fluidity, adoption of new technology, and a focus on upskilling. We'll get into more specifics later in this section.

We're also seeing some of the pain of change: fear of AI taking our jobs, return to office mandates or more employee surveillance tech to give leaders a greater sense of control, waves of layoffs, a rocky road for commercial real-estate markets, high employee turnover rates, mismatched expectations across generations causing strife, and dropping employee engagement and company loyalty.

Having some background in what's happening around us can help you navigate the shifting seas and get more benefits out of this changing world of work. Specifically, there are three trends that are changing how work will get done over the next decade:

1. Flexibility and autonomy
2. AI and upskilling
3. Productivity and measuring performance

Chapter 11
Flexibility & Autonomy

TLDR—Nine-to-five and cookie-cutter cubicles? Check the rearview mirror. Work is getting more flexible, BUT it can be tricky. This chapter will show you how to make flexibility work for you, and why how you work matters more than where. Learn how to build trust and sell your skills so you can unlock more control over your work and thrive in the future of work.

Flexibility Is Not a Perk

Much of the professional worker's job—digesting, creating, organizing, assessing, and sharing data and information—can now be done remotely. Thank you internet, the Cloud, Zoom, and the thousands of apps we use every day.

No longer does work HAVE to be done together at the same time in the same place. This gives us so many advantages. Asynchronous work takes advantage of flexing across different places, schedules, and timezones. That can be good for companies (more productivity) and good for the individual (flexibility). Flexibility is now a reality, not a perk.

The trick is this variance in time management and coordination also makes everything more complex. And we haven't quite figured all of that complexity out yet to make the most of this set of advantages. Hence some of the wild swings we've seen by companies going fully remote or not, then reversing the other direction, then landing somewhere in the middle, only to shift again. The best solution isn't here yet, and companies will shift again . . . and again, especially over the coming years.

On one side, the costs of using in-person office spaces are high:

- Working at the office averages about two times the cost of working remotely for each employee[xxix]
- Commercial real estate isn't cheap either; it's typically the second-highest cost behind paying employees[xxx]
- Many people find that working from home is more efficient because they convert commute time to something more productive and have more control over their environment, reducing distractions
- Opening more remote positions helps organizations expand their talent pool and hire more diversely, which leads to more people able to find meaningful work overall

On the other side, while the benefits of in-person collaboration[xxxi] in an office or physical space may be harder to put a hard number on, they are nonetheless big:

- Better onboarding and upskilling training
- Increases institutional knowledge sharing

- Creates more connection and trust-building between coworkers
- Fosters more mentorship opportunities
- Increases those "aha moments" of serendipity from informal hallway chats and a stronger feeling of "mission contagion" or being "in it" together

These are all ways in-office time can increase our sense of meaning in work.[xxxii] Post-pandemic many employees suffered from burnout and loneliness after endless Zoom meetings that lacked those informal connection moments. And let's not forget the power of proximity bias that creeps into performance reviews, rewarding in-office time (fair or not). Taken all together, interacting in-person can increase the chances of making more money, getting more opportunities, and feeling our work is meaningful.

Pro Tip: Make the most of your time wherever you're working. Given both remote and in-person work environments have benefits, take a moment to think about what you're getting out of your work and collaboration time and how you can lean into the benefits when available.

Remote & Distributed Work

Are you working fully remote? Or even just working on a distributed team with your manager and other team members in different locations? Then part of your job is to find ways to show up well. Not in your job description? Probably not, but trust me, the benefits are worth it.

Insider Truth: It's true. The rumor that fully remote workers are less likely to get promoted or be able to use internal mobility to get new job opportunities is in fact what often happens. Proximity bias is a strong influence on career success. This trend is even worse for women. Women are less likely to get access to new opportunities and pay raises when they don't benefit from mentoring relationships and proximity.

Good communications, giving meaningful visibility to your work, and seeking out supportive feedback and mentoring relationships (even virtual) are all great ways to combat this.

If you work remotely (or even just in a different office from your manager), be proactive about making connections and getting visibility for your work:

- **Schedule time:** invite people to (virtual) coffee chats, wellness hours, etc. that help you: 1) build relationships with coworkers, mentors, etc. and 2) help you learn about company culture outside of day-to-day work (ask about what's helped them be successful, what to avoid, etc.).
- **Communicate regularly:** Never assume people know what you're doing and where you've had success, especially if you're working remotely. Find ways to give visibility to your work (see chapter 13 for tips) and make sure you're regularly documenting your work and outcomes for your manager. Out of sight, out of mind—unfortunately this is for real the case, and something remote workers should be aware of.
- **Travel to an office:** If given the chance and budget, take the opportunity to go into an office or coworking space. Getting together with coworkers for onboarding, a planning meeting, project kickoff event, customer meeting, etc. is valuable.

Meeting people face-to-face will help establish a more solid foundation for trust and help them remember you better.

Insider Truth: Employers usually won't allow temporary remote work relocation for more than 30 days—a.k.a. working across state lines or abroad. Tax laws, data and privacy security concerns, and government or partnership compliance measures are all reasons why organizations need workers to have a consistent work location. Work from home isn't the same as remote work—and neither allow for location hopping. Lying to (or hiding from) your employer about where you're working can get you fired.

For those with in-office time, if you're going through the stress and cost of a commute and all that goes with it, make the most of it. Here's what the research suggests:

- **Early career research:** At the start of our careers we benefit from more exposure to seeing how work gets done, investing deeply in building relationships, learning about our roles in close proximity to others who have more experience or institutional knowledge. These are all reasons why studies show that more office time early in your career helps you be more successful throughout your career.
- **Mid-career research:** As we get more experience, we often feel less personal benefit from office time. Still, in-person time is good for team building and career development. It can help you form stronger mentorships as well as see what's going on in areas of the company outside of your current role so that you can make connections and take advantage of opportunities for building your career.

Skills-Based & Fractional Work

Flexibility is not just about *where* work gets done but *how*. These days more organizations are experimenting with skills-based models of work (vs. a reliance on pedigreed credentials).[xxxiii] This focus on matching skills to business problems creates a much bigger range of ways workers can create value. Here are some examples:

- **Internal Talent Marketplaces:** Organizations carve out time from employees' core roles so they can take on projects or tasks based on transferable skills.
- **Skills Hubs:** Organizations form a centralized team with a mix of skills that can be deployed to a variety of business problems as they arise.
- **Broadening Jobs:** Organizations loosen traditional job descriptions and metrics of success to allow workers to more holistically solve problems.

The benefits can go both ways. Skills-based work gives employees more exposure to a variety of work AND helps employers maximize employee skill sets to close skill gaps. All of the examples above mirror ways workers are already using fractional work (or project and task-based work) to create value and get paid for it. Think: freelancing, gig work, entrepreneurship. These are all examples of how people are increasingly working to use more of their skills to their own advantage. But the downside to fractional work outside an organization is the need to manage your own accounts, marketing, customer service, health benefits, etc. If organizations can successfully apply skills-based models internally, workers get the double advantage of having more options to create value with the benefits that come with a full-time job.

A New Dynamic

My prediction is that we'll find a new collaboration dynamic for *where* and *how* we work. We will recenter in-person time around more purposeful, meaningful interactions (like onboarding, training, planning onsites, annual or quarterly company performance reviews, project or product kickoff design sessions, etc.). This allows companies to downsize on some office space over time (saving money) and gives employees more flexibility and support for well-being, while also ensuring employees connect and build relationships around meaningful parts of company and employee development.

We'll also see more opportunities for workers to mix it up—what work they do and how they do it—based on their portfolio of skills. Whether taking a fractional approach to work within an organization (doing skills-based project work) or externally (as a gig worker or entrepreneur), most workers today will have a much more fluid career than previous generations. That means workers will need to know how to present their skills portfolio to their best advantage.

Pro Tip: Having a solid understanding of your "skills portfolio" is a must. I recommend using concentric circles of skills to model this. For example:

- **Core skills** (at the center): these skills are the foundation of your functional role
- **Differentiated skills** (expanding out): these skills set you apart and help you specialize
- **Potential skills** (outer circle): these are the skills you can develop to grow in influence or scope

How about an example from a skills maven?

Cheng's been working in human resources (HR)—also called the People team—for about five years. She started out as an HR generalist but knows the path to growing in the HR field means she needs to develop both specialist and leadership skills. Here's her concentric circles of skills outline:

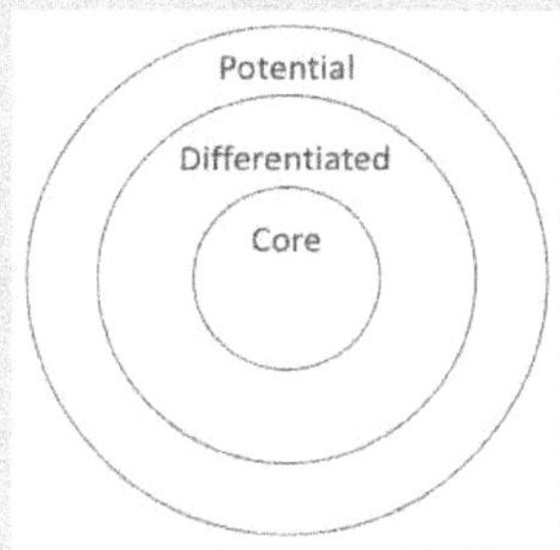

Core: understanding business management (e.g., employee policies and laws), interpersonal communication, judgment and decision-making, facilitation, empathy and conflict resolution

Differentiated: project management (for People Operations) and tooling (HRIS management)

Potential: business acumen and delegation (leadership)

Summary: Cheng has volunteered in the past to manage a project that involved HRIS (Human Resources Information System) data input as well as working with the Finance Department on translating business goals to headcount planning. The project helped her practice delegation and required her to ramp up on business model terminology. These are skills she can showcase and build on.

In your personal career map from Section One—Know Your Worth, you wrote down your skills and experiences. Take a quick look back at that list to assess which are core, differentiated, or potential skills that enhance your portfolio.

Large, well-established organizations—like that cruise liner—could take many years to make this shift. Some industries may continue to place more emphasis on in-person time and traditional job structures than others. Up-and-coming organizations with the freedom to build something new may embrace remote work altogether, skills-based models, or create new ways of working with flexibility. Regardless of where and how you work, I don't recommend taking flexibility for granted. Why? The key word here is trust—trust that goes both ways between employers and employees. And these days, trust and loyalty are at all-time lows.[xxxiv]

Autonomy Needs Trust

Our need for flexibility is rooted in a deeper desire for autonomy. We want the freedom and respect to choose how to approach our work. We want choice and input on when and where we work as well as how we make decisions, set project goals and just get things done.

When employers don't trust employees, we see them tighten control mechanisms and give less autonomy. Some examples: tighter policies (like: strict return-to-office mandates), more tracking (like: badging clock-in or monitoring of computer use), lack of equal opportunity for remote workers (like: lower rates of internal mobility or promotion), and general micromanagement. And vice-versa, when employees don't trust employers, you'll see a drop in loyalty. This can show up in many ways: job hopping, quiet quitting, burnout, lower quality of work, people leaving to take their chances with self-employment, etc. The environment this creates is not good for our well-being.

Great employers will work hard to build trust with their employees. Look for organizations who can share concrete examples of how they are investing in employee well-being, development, and clear flexibility guidelines or new models of skills-based work. At the same time, know that putting in effort to build trust with your employer can also go a long way.

Pro Tip: Taking proactive steps to build trust with your manager and organization can win you autonomy in return—freeing you to do your best work, how you best do it. Here are some ways to build trust while making it easier to get your work done:

- Take time to make sure you're aligned with your manager and team on shared goals (section two)
- Build strong relationships for collaboration
- Define the structure and boundaries that help you do your best work (e.g., focus time blocks, project milestones, etc.)—then get signoff (or adjust as needed) with your manager and team so they know what to expect and can partner with you better
- Give visibility to work that offers strong data and examples of what you can accomplish
- Show up as reliable or consistent

Doing this? Fab! You're greatly increasing your chances of getting more autonomy and more of what you need.

It's time to re-examine traditional structures in our changing landscape of work. Part of that change is placing autonomy and trust up front. Don't wait for your organization to figure it all out. To navigate the trust problem at the heart of this debate you can show (don't just tell your manager) why you deserve the autonomy to drive your work—and get more of the flexibility and well-being support you need.

Tools: Personal Career Map | Build for Your Future (Step 1: Build Trust, Create More Autonomy—5-min.): Free download here: www.jomcrell.com/free

Congrats!! You're on the last section. Time to protect your future and explore new ways you can get the flexibility you need. Pull out your copy of the personal career map, and then take a moment to move around and streeeetch because your future needs lots of space to grow.

Let's focus on **Step 1 and Flexibility first.**

Being visible and creating trust is the way to get more autonomy and the flexibility and well-being support that goes with it. Take a moment to write down two ways you can show up with your team consistently.

Chapter 12

Artificial Intelligence & Upskilling

TLDR—We need to make AI our teammate, not our enemy. To do that, we'll all need to brush up on new digital skills AND our human magic. If chapter 11 showed us how to organize a skills portfolio, this chapter is all about building those skills out for the future.

We started this section of the book feeling some #futureofwork wobbles. The disruption of generative artificial intelligence (GenAI) is a significant part of that wobble. Feeling a bit freaked out? Were you an early adopter of ChatGPT? Good. A little of both is OK. But before you get too excited or freaked out, let's ground ourselves in this essential truth: AI is a tool. And that means the most important question is: *How will you use AI to make your life better?*

I bet you're wondering . . . Did I use GenAI to write this book? Great question! Yes, you betcha! I used it in multiple ways—research, playing with content ideas, editing, publishing plan, etc. But AI was not good enough yet to compose the structure, stories, and examples or voice and tone that I wanted. Beyond that, GenAI tools like

ChatGPT, Gemini, and Perplexity AI aren't necessarily prioritizing the latest trends and research. There's also something else that AI doesn't have yet—actual work experience. So, useful? Yes! A replacement for you or me? No. Let's check back in a few years from now. . . .

What Is AI Anyway?

Backing up the truck for a minute, let's get specific about what we're talking about when we say AI. AI is artificial intelligence, or a computer model that uses a large data set trained to solve a specific kind of problem. You've likely used it when you open your phone using face ID, your computer pulls a date and place from an email and auto-creates a calendar event, or you ignore all the junk your email spam filter has pulled out.

GenAI is next level. GenAI is all about creating new or unique content—words, sounds, or images. GenAI goes beyond the immediate rules it's programmed to learn. It learns as it goes, creating new patterns or new variations. That's what makes it more human-like. A text-to-image generator is a great example and a lot of fun. Whatever you thought of the first AI generated music video "Betrayed by this Town" by Anna Indiana, the world's first all AI singer and songwriter, it was a pretty incredible first example of what GenAI could do.

Regardless, AI is a disruptive (vs. incremental) technology like: harnessing fire, the wheel, farming, steel, the printing press, personal computers, the internet, smartphones. Whenever we create disruptive tech there's always some good and some bad. It's about how we use it. Regardless, it's disruptive because it changes not only how we work but what work we do—and beyond that how we relate to one another. Rightly so, all this "human-like" capability with GenAI has people worried. Putting a potential apocalypse aside, one of people's biggest worries is losing their job to automation. Overall, the goal will be to do more with fewer resources (like humans) . . . but also to do new things (that humans are needed for). There's definitely downside as well as upside.

AI's Impact on Jobs

There is no doubt that AI will bring significant change to professionals or knowledge-based workers.[xxxv] Yep. That means you and me. In past economic revolutions, machines and tech automated a lot of manual or blue-collar work. Think: GPS self-driving combines harvesting grain in agriculture or robot welders in car manufacturing factories. This time around the biggest impact is on automating knowledge-based or white-collar work. Automation today is centered on the organization, production, and distribution of information.

Technology revolutions have always disrupted jobs. This will be more of the same—but faster. In some cases AI technology is eliminating jobs, dramatically changing others, creating new jobs, and making others even more important than they were before. Check out some of the most common examples to see where your skills net out.

Examples of work likely to be increasingly automated and therefore have less need for humans to directly perform it:

- **Administrative**—sending basic communications, handling correspondence, scheduling meetings, creating summaries
- **Coding**—writing code, creating sub-programs, searching large coding databases to solve programming problems

- **Content Generation**—creating summaries, writing new content, generating images as well as voiceovers and video
- **Customer Service**—giving personalized responses to customer questions, gauging sentiment, call routing, translation, complaint-trend analysis
- **Finance**—reviewing transactions, analyzing financial data, creating predictive reports, tax and payroll calculations
- **Human Resources**—sourcing candidates, reviewing résumés, applying chat bots for internal self-serve on benefits, and other programs
- **Legal**—document review, contract analysis, research, and case law references
- **Operations**—analyzing data, creating reports and insights, reviewing processes
- **Sales and Marketing**—generating sales outreach, identifying upsell and cross-sell opportunities, drafting and sending marketing campaigns
- **Training and Development**—personalizing development paths, generating learning modules, sending coaching tips

This type of automation will definitely impact lots of jobs. Some estimates say up to 12 million jobs will be automated by 2030.[xxxvi] For context, there are about 150 million adults working in the US each year, so that'd be about 8% of jobs. However, many more jobs will be reshaped or updated. In many cases, AI may automate key tasks or parts of a job but not entire functions or roles. The promise is AI disruption will reduce the amount of repetitive and boring work we have to do. This is what people call "augmentation." Augmenting is when tech like AI supports humans and helps them do more or better work. In this case, it's called "augmented intelligence." Either way, no matter where this lands, we're all going to need to adapt to new tools and ways of working.

So what types of skills or jobs will AI create more demand for? Glad you asked, 'cause it looks like lots of potential in multiple areas:

- **Top job fields in demand for the future**: Healthcare and mental health, green energy, data science, operations analytics, information or cyber security, software development, artificial intelligence and machine learning, digital marketing, logistics, construction, management analytics
    - Note that a lot of these jobs are about using data to make business operations more efficient—making companies more money or saving it. (Sound familiar?! If not, see chapter 3.)
    - I'm also sure there will be whole new job categories (like prompt engineering) over the next decade, so always be on the lookout for new opportunities!
- **Top skills in demand for the future**: Technical and STEM, analytical thinking and problem-solving, communication, creativity, resilience and adaptability, emotional intelligence, leadership, developing relationships and teamwork, entrepreneurship, self-management (like goal setting and time management)
    - Note: Digital skills are a must, yes, AND see the number of people skills on the list? Make sure you're setting yourself up with both.
- **More entrepreneurship:** AI is automating more of the data analysis and tasks needed to run a business (inventory management, basic digital marketing, tax calculations, etc.). This can free up business owners to more quickly explore and create new products, services, and models for their business. Learning AI tools and skills can help you develop a valuable side hustle that could become your ultimate dream job.

Insider Truth: Women are more likely to be disrupted by AI automation than men in professional roles. That's because women tend to hold more of the administrative, customer service, and content-generation jobs that AI automates so well. When more women than men are impacted, laid off, or not even hired, it becomes a self-fulfilling prophecy that men are more "skilled."

This is why it's even more important for women to not only invest in upskilling but to also create visibility when we upskill to avoid bias and replacement strategies. Same is true here for people of color.

Bottom Line: AI is only as good as the data we give it. While it has the capacity to crunch through a LOT more data than humans, it's also susceptible to garbage in, garbage out (hello AI hallucinations). And AI applications are limited by the rules and patterns used to train them. We humans have a wider range of possible inputs—life experience, emotional cues, observation, creativity, etc. We will still need to define what good looks like—in the context of human society at large, as well as for more daily decisions like when and how to apply an AI tool to a project. I have a lot of faith in the opportunity for us humans to continue creating value and getting paid for it. We'll just need to learn some new tricks along the way.

Pro Tip: Since AI is itself on the fast-track—growing and evolving seemingly by the week—most of us are learning as we go. Find a safe community to experiment with, share tips, and explore new tools. This can be just as valuable as more formal AI training.

Upskilling Beyond AI

It's not just AI disruption that's changing the skills needed today. There are lots of reasons employers are updating the skill sets they are looking for: more distributed workforces, continued need for basic STEM skills, larger macroeconomic change and flux, more diverse and multigenerational workforces, more contextualized business problems (example: increasing pressure to create products and services with environment, social, community impact in mind—YAY!), a restructuring education system, etc. So what can you do to secure your success for your future?

Balance your skill sets: While hard and digital skills are a must to get you in the door, people skills are how you smooth your path, advance, and just love your work a little more. So, yes, digital skills are a must, AND employers are increasingly prioritizing hires who demonstrate adaptability, resilience, growth mindset, people leadership, judgment/decision-making, emotional intelligence and relationship building, etc. Your people skills could be your differentiator.

- Much has been made about Gen Z lacking key people skills. This is a bit of a cop-out. Every generation has complained about the generation after it. Moving on . . . what is important for all of us is learning some cultural dexterity. Whether that's to help you work across generations from Zoomers to Boomers or because most organizations have a mix of people from different cultures and backgrounds, being able to flex your people skills is very helpful.

Balance for human-machine collaboration: GenAI has the promise to shift our work mix and make our work more meaningful. It can automate boring, repetitive tasks and help you with your more complex work. Here's a two-step approach to thinking about AI as a way to augment your intelligence:

- **Step 1: AI or human needed?** First, do a task breakdown for your day-to-day work. Then for each task, decide whether AI can automate that task, augment or assist you in doing the task, or whether the task requires your unique human capabilities.
- **Step 2: Update your work mix**! This is all about shifting your effort and focus to make the most out of the work you do AND safeguard your relevance in the future of work. You can think about work being three types of activities: transactional (tasks), relational (building relationships and collaborating), and transformational (applying expertise). Today, the average work mix for knowledge-based workers is about 50% transactional, 30% relational, and 20% transformational. Studies estimate we should get a 10-30% increase in productivity in the coming years from applying AI to our work mix.[xxxvii] By automating tasks and using AI to assist you with your more complicated work, you should aim to cut your transactional work by over 50%. That also gives you more time (almost double) to increase your more valuable relational and transformational work. Or do less work (for less time) and still increase the value you create.

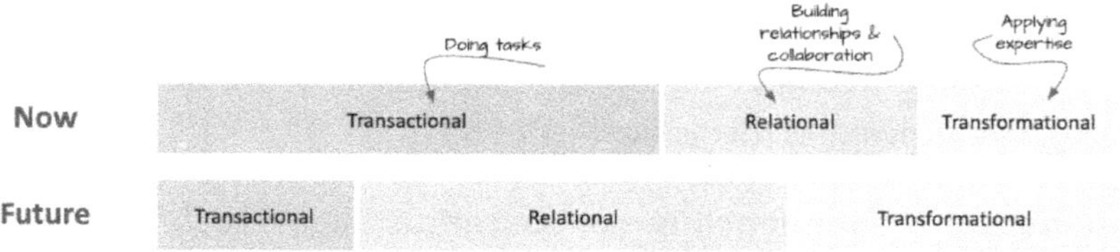

Now is the time to start experimenting. Use the tools, thinking about what you can automate in your job to free up time and energy for more strategic or interesting work. Explore online courses to learn something new (like: prompt design, content creation, search bots, self-service implementations). Try applying new tools to an existing work project. Learning by doing can be the best way to motivate yourself and speed your way to a new skill set.

Insider Truth: AI's data gathering and crunching capabilities will be put to work monitoring you. Departments like Finance and HR will increasingly use applications built to streamline processes or make things more efficient. You'll see apps offering personalized services like coaching and development, training modules, tracking goals and progress, or identifying high-stress moments in your workday and offering up mental health resources. There are benefits to this. However, it's likely that this monitoring will increasingly impact how performance is measured. Pay attention to what data is being collected about you.

Balance for long-term output: Remember talking about goals in chapter 3? I hope so! Well, it's a good idea to keep an eye on your priorities and refresh your long-term goals every couple of years. The idea is to always be learning—AND make it goal oriented so it's not just about the quantity of what you can do but the quality of the value you can create.

We already talked about how most people change jobs 12-plus times. Now we're changing careers at least a few times during our lives. Career coaches and leaders used to advise people to reinvent themselves every 3-5 years—looking for that next chapter in their career. Now it's much more realistic to tighten that up to every 2-3 years. Often you'll be focused on upskilling. At some point, you might need to reskill and pivot in a whole new direction.

Where and how can you upskill or reskill? There might be opportunities both in-house where you work as well as externally, but don't wait for your employer to offer the training you need if you're ready to upskill. Be on the lookout for a variety of ways to learn:

- **Upskilling**: Formal educational institutions like colleges and universities are still important but not agile enough to support all the training and upskilling needed. Look for online credentialed courses (examples: LinkedIn Learning, Coursera, edX, Codecademy, Udacity), apprenticeship programs, community college programs, or short-term / role-specific training programs like boot camps. Even better if the course offers an evaluation or helps you develop a work product so you can show (vs. tell) employers what your new skills are.
- **Reskilling**: At some point you might need to change industries, job functions, or just hit reset on your career path altogether. Putting your toes in the water by volunteering before making the switch is one option—either within your current organization or externally. Some companies offer rotation programs to help employees explore new role types. You might also take a temporary position or enroll in a job-specific training program. There's also growing attention and investment in apprenticeships (and not just for new grads).[xxxviii] Regardless, make sure you assess two things: 1) skills you already have that you can transfer to your new career path and 2) evidence that the reskilling option you invest in has led others to a successful transition.

- **"New-collar" work**: These are jobs that need advanced skills but not necessarily advanced degrees. These opportunities are mushrooming in emerging fields like artificial intelligence, cybersecurity, green tech, and robotics. I think we'll continue to see new-collar fields expand into even traditional industries like healthcare and digital marketing as employers focus more and more on skills-based hiring. This way of approaching work creates new options with more agile, focused learning than a traditional four-year degree.

Tools: Personal Career Map | Build for Your Future (Step 2: Upskilling—5-min. exercise): Free download here: www.jomcrell.com/free

There's nothing better for reducing anxiety than taking action. By looking ahead and regularly checking in with yourself on the skills you're investing in, you are increasing your value and career options at the same time!

OK, **Step 2: Upskilling**. Stay curious and learn something new. This not only supercharges your career options but just makes life and work more interesting. Make sure you write down concrete options for taking action on the skill you're interested in.

Reminder: There are so many ways to learn; it doesn't have to be formal training or boring business books (unlike this one ;)). Keep your eyes open for shadowing, podcasts, online modules, etc. Feeling stressed about adding more to your schedule? One of the best and easiest ways to learn is to apply new skills to one of your existing projects. Just keep in mind whether you need some kind of official credential to convert that skill into higher pay.

When you look to your future, I hope you see a lot of possibilities. Because there are SO many possibilities. That's part of the beauty of change. Where there is change, there is opportunity. In a way, there are so many different opportunities opening up that it can be overwhelming. Don't let your head explode with all the info, all the hype, all the opinions. If you've put in the effort to narrow in on your priorities and goals (sections one and two), then AI and all the other skills you'll need to polish or learn just become tools that make your work easier and supercharge your success.

[Extra] Recommended Resource: *Quantum Progression: The Art & Science of Career Advancement in the Age of A.I.* by Valerie Capers Workman

Chapter 13

The Productivity Crisis

TLDR—Work smarter, not harder. Heard this one before? Likely, but I doubt you're getting much support to make it happen. Our work culture has rewarded busywork for far too long. Let's work together to find better ways to show impact and manage our energy for a performance that impresses the boss (and more importantly helps us love our work now and in the future!).

The previous chapters on flexibility, AI, and upskilling are part of the equation here for what I'm calling the "productivity crisis." What makes it a "crisis?" Lots of disruptive forces are colliding all at the same time. I'll boil it down to the big three:

- **Employee experience disruption**: Employees are changing their expectations and new needs are creating a cultural disruption with a move toward more autonomy, flexibility and a focus on well-being.

- **Technology disruption**: GenAI is pushing us into a new era of technology and therefore new ways of working and interacting.
- **Economic disruption**: Our economy is dealing with inflation, conflicts, climate impact, skill gaps and more. Not only that, but more and more the economy is being driven by value created online (Sharing and Creative Economies) vs. the physical world—another disruption.

Companies are now ultra-focused on increasing productivity as the number one driver of their business plans.[xxxix] No shocker here. The result is the ways companies used to measure productivity, and therefore our own individual performance, have to change.

Productivity under Pressure

Productivity is constantly under pressure to go up. Leaders feel this pressure—to reduce the cost of running their organization while increasing the value they create. And this pressure gets passed down . . . all the way to you. I imagine you're feeling this pressure in some form. Global polls of workers tell us Americans are some of the most stressed employees in the world.[xl]

When work is disrupted because of new tools and innovations, economists and business leaders expect to see the productivity of each worker go up and the focus of their work to evolve. We've seen this trend in past eras—from the Agricultural to Industrial to the Information Age—major economic revolutions disrupted how work was done and what type of work we humans got paid for. After all, the idea behind any tool is to do more with fewer resources.

But here's the challenge. Since the 1970s, we've been seeing not more productivity but less. This drop is despite so many advances in tech—like the internet or having a supercomputer—a.k.a. smartphone—in our pockets.[xli] Add onto that the emergence of GenAI, and the pressure cooker around productivity to climb back up is getting hot!

Insider Truth: Post-pandemic many companies and leaders blamed a drop in productivity on things like remote work. They began leaning back into old measures of productivity and success. They're tempted by the idea that having people physically come into an office will automatically increase what each person accomplishes, improve company culture, and raise the bottom line. Monkey see, monkey do. Hmmmm. . .

Most leaders understand the reality is a lot more complicated and that we have to evolve how we work, what work we value, and how we measure the productivity of both. But it's easier said than done and will take a number of years for many companies to not only redefine productivity but to also rework their systems and processes to support this change.

Busywork Is Out

Traditional productivity metrics are a big part of the problem because they're often focused on transactional activity. For example: tracking working hours, number of bugs fixed, number of customer service calls answered, or the amount of data entered, etc. After all, activity is much easier to track and has more standards around it. When you add all of this emphasis on tracking activity to the sheer amounts of information and data that have been part of the Information Age, you get something many of us are all too familiar with—busywork. To be busy in corporate America has become synonymous with being productive. It's a norm. It's hustle culture. It's a way for leaders to feel reassured "things are happening." It's our own reaction to FOMO. But it's also why so many employees say they feel like "cogs in a wheel"—a very Industrial or Manufacturing Age analogy instead of an Information Age experience of value.

Let's take one example: Just look at the number of forum posts, blogs, Slack discussions, and LinkedIn articles complaining about death by meetings. How many times have we gone through a day of meetings, to write notes on those meetings, to then be asked to create a presentation summarizing what was covered in those meetings so that we can have another meeting to discuss it. Raise your hand if this sounds familiar. Yep, my hand is up. I definitely fell into this trap of busy = productive (a.k.a. proof that I'm valuable).

Busy is not going to cut it anymore. With technology automating more and more of that transactional activity or tactical work (hello, AI!), it's losing its value.

Beyond this challenge, there's a very human side to the transactional work problem: boredom and frustration. We don't do very well when our work is quantity over quality. When it's the same old, same old every day. Or when it feels meaningless. When it doesn't maximize our creative thought power. When we're so busy we don't have time to eat lunch, and yet at the end of the week, we find ourselves wondering what the hell we got done. Hello, burnout!

The macro pressure on productivity at the company-wide level shows up for us individual professionals in our performance metrics. The challenge today is that our more complex work involving creativity, problem-solving, or strategic decision-making is not assessed well using traditional productivity metrics. However, it's worth your time and energy to understand how to measure your performance for that more valuable work.

Measuring Impact & Energy Is In

So measuring your performance to demonstrate productivity is a problem. AND it's your problem. Opportunity alert! It can also be a way for you to stand out. Good news. We've already talked about one great way to demonstrate your value and productivity. Remember all that stuff about goals and documentation from section two? Awesome! 'Cause sharing the same expectations with your manager, setting actionable personal goals, and documenting everything well gives you a huge leg up. And having clear personal goals will go a loooooong way toward making you feel that your work is meaningful—a great productivity metric as you track your own well-being.

Now two more—let's talk about **impact** and **energy management**. Starting with **impact**: this is all about outcome metrics and showing how you can solve important problems. After all, showcasing your awesome skills portfolio to get awesome work opportunities is great, but getting the rewards for applying those skills and creating valuable impact is better! There are multiple things you can do to create and demonstrate more impact:

Align your work to business goals

- In section three we covered the basics of business acumen—that the primary focus for businesses is to make and save money. If you didn't add it then, now is the time to go back to your Section Two: Create Value in your Personal Career Map and look for ways to help make more money and/or save it in pursuit of your top goals. This could be using better tools, learning how to better manage your time, innovating on the processes involved, etc. Got some ideas here? Love it!
- Your organization may use a goal and outcomes framework—like objectives and key results (OKRs), key performance indicators (KPIs), or a set of benchmarks. Regardless of what the framework is, learning how to frame your goals and impact in that way can help shortcut your way to alignment.

Align on the key outcome metrics

- Share your ideas with your manager and team. Use these conversations to get aligned on the outcome metrics that are most important to them and your function (like a new product feature coded at a certain quality level, a policy updated to better support and reflect specific evolving employee needs, or customer cases closed with a high level of satisfaction). Getting the idea that this is more about quality than quantity of outcome? Excellent!

Document your impact

- To show you're a high performer, make sure you're documenting the impact of your work—not just your goals and steps to get there. You can include both quantitative metrics (the numbers like money made or saved) AND qualitative outputs (like customer testimonials, glowing stakeholder feedback).

Insider Truth: You may see more AI in performance-management applications that offer personalized coaching for development and goal setting. It may also assess feedback and help HR and leaders see trends that will shape their own understanding of "good" performance across groups of employees.

Keep in mind this use of AI is new and evolving. Make sure you continue to check in with your manager on how they define "good" as well so that well-intentioned AI suggestions don't steer you off course.

Let's get an example from marketing: At the beginning of the year, Marla in online marketing sat down with her manager to define her six-month goals. She expected a version of what she'd done for the last year or so—tracking campaigns against number of clicks, downloads, and the amount of social media posts plus engagement on those. But Marla's manager had a different idea.

They asked Marla to start by defining the goal. In their case they needed to bring in more leads or potential customers to test the freemium version of their product. Given this goal, Marla worked with her Revenue Operations team to set a new outcome-based metric: increase clicks to freemium sign-up buttons by 25%.

With this outcome in mind, Marla changed how she worked. She planned more tests to see which keywords generated more freemium clicks. She worked with the User Experience (UX) team to study potential customers in more depth and created targeted campaigns to help different kinds of customers understand their product's value. At the end of six months, Marla had created fewer posts and overall clicks had gone down, but she surpassed the team's original numbers with an increase of 28% clicks to freemium signups. By refocusing on a clear goal and an outcome metric, Marla created more quality and impact (vs. quantity).

Impact is definitely tied to outcomes. But don't just think end work product. Showing the skills you've developed or improvements you've made to the work process along the way are also super valuable. Make sure you highlight those too! This is what they call measuring what matters. And as we learned in this section already, our most valuable work will be focused more and more on relational and transformational work—not the transactional or tactical stuff AI can help you take care of.

Pro Tip: Whether they say it or not, leaders are assessing their team members for the "human performance metrics" like relationship building, collaboration, influencing, learning and growth mindset, etc. That's because these skills have such a positive impact on teamwork and help everyone be more engaged and productive.

Getting ahead of this by making it a part of your goals and outcome tracking will help you shape the story with your manager AND help you shine. Create the most compelling story with this focus on strategic, human-powered impact!

In Marla's story above, her collaboration with the Revenue Operations and UX teams also helped them show better numbers and showcased the value of what they produce (data and customer-use-case insights). By telling her story well, she reflects some of that goodness on them and builds stronger relationships.

OK. Now you're driving impact and everyone's feeling the value. Love it! But how are your energy levels? Let's talk **energy management**.

Traditionally, people talk about time management. And now with AI automating the heck out of lots of tasks, there's a resurgence in time-management tips and content. Still, this concept is a little outdated. You know because you've been there, right? Maybe you've been incredibly efficient squeezing in ten meetings and huddles a day, but by 4 p.m. your brain hurts, and you can't remember what you wanted to get done. Energy management is not just about the time you spend to get more things done. It's about understanding how to use your energy ebbs and flows to get better work done without sacrificing your well-being.

My friend Jackie. Jackie is a hustle culture OG. She is also a GenAI early adopter. Jackie uses AI to manage her calendar, organize her to-do lists, set up reminders, summarize her meetings, streamline her work flows, set up stakeholder emails, code her spreadsheets, and customize her workout at the end of the day. AI has helped her cram more into each day.

The trouble is that Jackie is worried about losing track of the people connected to her projects and her own sense of accomplishment. She's starting to feel the way she shows up to work discussions is sounding like a rinse-and-repeat exercise.

After talking to Jackie about her work life for 20 minutes, I could tell she was tired and getting lost in the details. Life was starting to feel like a blur of motion. We talked about the need to disrupt her current energy flow . . . as productive as it seemed. She agreed to slot in a morning and afternoon five-minute meditation pause and a midday slot for 30 minutes of reflection.

At first making the change raised Jackie's anxiety levels. *This is slowing me down. And I don't feel like it's making a difference.* But after a week of sticking with the plan, Jackie gained some insights about her energy levels. She found that when she stacked her mornings with meetings, she lost her ability to think creatively in the afternoon. She also found that when she added a walk to her midday reflection, she had more energy to deal with tough problems or coworker drama.

Armed with this insight, Jackie tested a new schedule the following week. She rebalanced her meetings across the day, got rid of a few meetings that could be chat-based, made sure she got in a daily walk, and (bonus!) added a 30 minute online learning course early in the week on a topic she was curious about. By the end of the week, she had created and pitched a new program idea to her manager and felt way more balanced overall.

Knowledge-based workers like us are valued for our ability to think. If we don't have healthy habits and proactively manage our energy, we risk creating our own personal energy crisis—and that is BAD for our thinking abilities. With AI checking more tactical tasks off the list, you might be hearing the phrase: *Do more with less!* But the real win here is to get more *with more*. More tool support. More healthy habits. More quality.

You can protect your energy levels and design a better workflow for your needs by checking in with yourself on these four key energy dimensions[xlii]:

- **Physical**: How are you doing on sleep, exercise, and nutrition? Even small adjustments around these three factors can create huge wins. Some well-researched ideas: add in a few moments of move and groove to your day, turn off devices one hour before bed, and substitute something healthy for a not-so-healthy snack.

- **Mental**: How do you create space for focus and minimize distractions? Switching your attention from one ping to the next can cost you 25% of your efficiency. Some well-researched ideas: Schedule in time to focus on a regular basis and turn off notifications. Decide on boundaries with your manager and team to communicate with respect or handle urgent items.
- **Emotional**: How do you respond to emotional triggers? Letting our emotions control us vs. us controlling them can be exhausting. Some well-researched ideas: take small breaks to create a positive interruption each day with meditation, breathing exercises, or to process negative interactions.
- **Spiritual**: How do you balance important work with your values and life priorities? Feeling that our time is spent in meaningful ways can have a BIG impact on our energy. Some well-researched ideas: Check back in on your priorities from section one to make sure you're focused on the right things, block more time for your most important activities, and be honest about what you're willing to trade off.

More and more companies are seeing the link between energy (or well-being) and performance (or productivity). We're continuing to see more investment in well-being benefits as well as just more conversations about health sponsored by leadership. Take advantage of what's offered! But since managing energy levels is a little different for everyone, check-in with yourself and make your own adjustments.

Tools: Personal Career Map |Build for Your Future (5 min. exercise): Free download here: www.jomcrell.com/free

This is IT! The last exercise of the last section. Get your productivity plan together, and you're ready for anything.

This is **Step 3**. Current self, say hello to future self. You're going to pick 1-2 key metrics that measure outcomes you create and that show impact. Follow that up with a new well-being habit you're going to try out to up your energy management game.

Got those down? It's time to CELEBRATE!!! You're on the way to making work work for you. I'm so excited for you!!!

Closing

Wowziers! We covered a lot of ground! From reassessing your priorities to navigating the plot twists of the changing workplace, you've now got the truth, tips, and tools about work you need to get more of what you want. I want you to have more choices so you can make better choices. That's the way to transform your work and create a career you love.

Let's recap the highlights from the book.

Make work *work* for you: We busted the myth that work should be a soul-sucking slog. This book empowered you to find meaning and purpose in your career, while also fueling your personal goals. You learned how to advocate for yourself, set boundaries, and build a work environment that supports your skills and passions.

Know your worth: You know now that your worth is more than a number or a paycheck. You learned how to identify your unique skills and experiences, research your market value, and negotiate for the total rewards you deserve. Remember, financial freedom gives you the power to make choices and pursue your dreams.

Create more value: You've found your career sweet spot and the crown is yours! Forget the one-size-fits-all approach to careers. This book helped you adapt your approach to avoid burnout, set action-packed goals, and identify the work environment that helps you thrive. You've got the people skills to protect your work, reduce bias, and bring more people into your inner circle of supporters.

Avoid common problems: Ugh! Workplace drama is the reality. This section equipped you with the skills to handle tough but all-too-common situations, from managing a bad boss to recovering from a career-limiting move. We explored the top workplace challenges and provided strategies to turn them into opportunities for growth.

Build for your future: Work is changing. Now you're ready to move forward and navigate both the challenges and opportunities. You know how to adapt not just where but how you work to get more flexibility, autonomy, and trust. You're confident you can make AI your teammate, not your enemy. You can showcase your skills and upskill with the best of them. And maybe most importantly, you're making valuable impact without sacrificing your energy and well-being.

You are NOT alone in this journey! Work can be complex and ever-changing, but with the truth, tips, and tools from this book, you can cut through the noise and focus on what empowers you.

Here are some final words of encouragement (and tough love)!

Believe in yourself. Be honest with yourself. Be confident. Get specific so you can follow through. Take the time to hone your people skills (more!). Be replaceable. Know that bias happens, so work on your counter strategy. Don't do stupid $hit (that can be avoided). Keep learning. Have fun.

I know that you've got this! Hey. You've read this book, so I know you're thinking, you're motivated, you're doing something. That's a great start!

If (instead) you've skipped to the end to see if it's worth reading, OK. I got you. Skip around. Check out the books and resources I referenced that other fantabulous women have shared. Whatever works.

You own your career success. You decide.

Whatever you do, get some truth—especially since the world of work is full of myths, and what was true a few years ago is not the same now. Put some tools in your toolbox. Find people you admire who can share good tips. And then make choices. Good choices. Choices that make work *work* for you.

Acknowledgements

No meaningful effort is undertaken alone. This book is no exception. From the first moment I began wondering aloud about the idea of writing it, I was surrounded by people who supported and championed this work. Many had experienced pain in their own careers. Some were driven by allyship. Others have dedicated their own expertise to shaping our new era of work.

I exited this book writing process exhausted *and* energized! Turns out writing a whole book—and worse yet, editing it—is hard work! But above all, I'm grateful. There is a strong spirit of incredible community in this book.

My deepest gratitude goes to my extraordinary content editing team. I asked for hard graders and got that and much more—incredible subject-matter expertise, encouragement, new perspectives, reminders of my fallacies and strengths, and *most of all* shared enthusiasm for empowering you—the reader. Thank you to the team: Michele McGovern, tenured journalist and editor specializing in HR trends; Logan Rizzo, audience expert and communications master; Paulina Houston, employment law and employee advocacy expert; and Liz Wilke, economist specializing in labor trends.

I'm also grateful for all the curious people who volunteered to be sounding boards and beta readers, even when the book was still rough around the edges. Thank you for believing in my audience and carving time aside to think about what would make this book more helpful, more relevant to a diverse set of people, and (super important!) more interesting: Bernard C. Coleman III, Colleen Flaherty, Eileen Fagan, Emily Hecker, Elise Pereira, Jazz Samra, Jessica Virk, Jen Tanabe, Kelly Monahan, Laura Holden, Lauren Harris, Misty Schachtell-Megia, Muoi Landivar, Nathalie Salles-

Oliver, Ronita Mondal, Shannon King, Tori Bell, William Chiu, and Yvette Huygen—all of you helped shape this book into something better.

I wouldn't have even thought to write a book if it hadn't been for those who inspired me with their own writing journeys. Rachel Richards, author of *Money Honey*, showed me what was possible with self-publishing and the power of women speaking up to empower other women. Chandler Bolt's book, *Published: The Proven Path From Blank Page To 10,000 Copies Sold*, gave me a way to move forward.

This book is also an opportunity for me to champion other women. Though I referenced these authors and creators throughout the book, they deserve additional shoutouts here: S. Lucia Kanter St. Amour, Rachel Richards (again!), Nancy Soni, Regina Lawless, Myriam Del Angel, Minda Harts, Alison Green, and Valerie Capers Workman.

A special thank you to Nadene Seiters, whose copy editing and formatting magic polished the manuscript to a shine. She's a great example of a woman making her own way on her own terms in the gig and creative economies. Mehmooda Sultana, your insightful cover design captured the book's essence, and your way of seeing the book visually helped me envision success.

Any errors caught by readers are on me. Left to my own devices, I'd probably make edits til my last breath—and did (a little) editing even after the book was declared "final." Ha! Nothing in life is ever final (wink, wink).

This is a non-fiction book written for professionals, but there's a great deal of the personal here. Work and life intertwines for all of us. My family and friends have been amazing.

I'm extremely lucky to have found my soulmate and married him. We have fought hard to be together, and it's been worth every moment. Uday, you gave me the space, time, and most importantly, the unwavering belief that I could and should write this book. You tolerated writer's block meltdowns and bursts of frenetic writing energy with (almost) endless patience and love. You also demanded that I get it done and move on with enjoying other things in life when I was at risk of endless edits. Thank you!

As the saying goes, "*When you're a kid, you don't realize you're also watching your parents grow up.*" Kiran you've taught me and helped me be a better person. Thank you for letting me learn with you as we built a family.

Speaking of parents, thank you to mine (Jim and Ellen), who showed me by example that great obstacles can be overcome with resilience, a commitment to community, and a spirit of adventure. I left home and traveled many places far away, but you've never left me.

Ruth, you welcomed our blended, multi-cultural family with open arms, endless curiosity, and the most enthusiastic cheerleading I could ask for. Everyone who comes in contact with you is blessed, and I'm so glad to be one of them.

. . . And thank you to the larger community around me. So many people have championed me along my own career journey (sometimes even when I was being stubbornly clueless or just stubborn!). Looking forward, I see so many people around me working hard to help shape the future of work—so that a bigger diversity of people can create more value for themselves and others. You are seen and appreciated!

And finally, but definitely not least, I'm grateful for you. You the reader. You are helping shape the future. My hope is that you shape a future full of choices, meaning, and hope. And from that place of strength, I encourage you to pay it forward—whether that's mentoring, sponsoring, just listening, sharing experiences, or advocating. You can also help more and more people find success on their own terms. Thank you!

About the Author

Jo McRell is an innovative employee experience strategist. She's helped organizations like Google, Intuit, Meta and Gusto better empower their employees. Jo understands the challenges young professionals face as the dynamics of the workplace change. Through her work and the AI ERA Community she co-founded, Jo equips employees and leaders with the tools to navigate tech, employee culture, and work model disruptions so they can thrive in the future of work. Jo is currently exploring California with her family and furry friend.

Glossary

1:1 Meeting—a meeting between your manager and you, often used as a status update and problem-solving meeting meant to keep the manager up to date and get you the support you need

AI—artificial intelligence (GenAI—generative artificial intelligence)

AI Hallucination—when AI creates misinformation or misleading results

a.k.a.—also known as

Bro Culture–an environment that prioritizes competitiveness to the point of exclusivity focused on youth, men, and often white people; the success of women and underrepresented people is considered an aberration; popularized in the tech and finance industries

BTW–by the way

CLM–career limiting move, a workplace issue that can get you fired or damage your reputation and limit your opportunities

Creative Economy—people making money out of creative ideas (rather than traditional resources like land, labor, and capitol); think YouTube influencer

CYA—cover your a$$

EQ—emotional intelligence

Flux—fluctuation

FOMO—fear of missing out

Fractional Work—a subcategory of the gig economy; hired for a fraction of your time, dividing your work time among multiple employers; less about project-based work and more as a part-time, expert resource; think Fractional Chief Human Resources Officer (CHRO)

Gig Work—working for a specific period of time or part-time (freelance, part-time, project-based); think Uber driver or a frontline medical staffer picking up shift work

IRL–in real life, in person

JK—just kidding

Jungle Gym—an analogy for career development that promotes taking a sideways role move at times instead of just trying to climb up the "corporate ladder"

New Collar—workers with advanced skills but not necessarily an advanced degree (e.g., college diploma)

OG—stands for original gangster; means authentic or expert

Pivot—changing or modifying your approach to try something that might work better

Sharing economy—economic model that's all about people collaborating to share goods, resources, and services; think home owner on Airbnb or an Etsy seller specializing in recycled vintage clothing

STEM—science, technology, engineering, and math

Total Rewards—base salary + benefits (including vacation and sick time off) + perks + any equity, commission, bonus, as well as programs that invest in employees like career development, flexibility, and well-being

WTF—what the f*ck

MY PLEA!

Thank you for reading my book!

I'd love to hear what you have to say and value your feedback. Your input will help make the next version of this book or the next project I work on better.

Please take two minutes now to leave a helpful review on Amazon: www.jomcrell.com/book-review

Thank you so much!

—Jo McRell

References

[i] Clockify; "Average Working Hours (Statistical Data 2023)"; https://clockify.me/working-hours.

[ii] The American Institute of Stress; "Workplace Stress"; https://www.stress.org/workplace-stress.

[iii] Fisher, Jen, Paul H. Silverglate, Colleen Bordeaux, and Michael Gilmartin. "As workforce well-being dips, leaders ask: What will it take to move the needle?" *Deloitte Insights* (blog), June 20, 2023, https://www2.deloitte.com/us/en/insights/topics/talent/workplace-well-being-research.html.

[iv] Harter, Jim ,"U.S. Employee Engagement Needs a Rebound in 2023," *Gallup* (blog), January 25, 2023, https://www.gallup.com/workplace/468233/employee-engagement-needs-rebound-2023.aspx.

[v] Ito, Aki, "The end of workplace loyalty," *Business Insider*, January 22, 2024, https://www.businessinsider.com/loyalty-employee-employer-job-security-broken-work-companies-bosses-2024-1.

[vi] Justworks; "2022 Health Insurance Knowledge Snapshot"; https://www.justworks.com/lp/benefits-knowledge-snapshot.

[vii] Madgavkar, Anu, Bill Schaninger, Sven Smit, Lola Woetzel, Hamid Samandari, Davis Carlin, Jeongmin Seong, and Kanmani Chockalingam. "Human capital at work: The value of experience," McKinsey & Company (blog), June 2, 2022, https://www.mckinsey.com/capabilities/people-and-organizational-performance/our-insights/human-capital-at-work-the-value-of-experience.

[viii] Maurer, Roy. "State by State: Salary History Bans and Pay Transparency Laws," *State of HR Management* (blog), August 23, 2023, https://www.shrm.org/resourcesandtools/hr-topics/talent-acquisition/pages/state-pay-equity-laws.aspx.

[ix] The University of Texas Permian Basin; "How Much of Communication Is Nonverbal?"; https://online.utpb.edu/about-us/articles/communication/how-much-of-communication-is-nonverbal/.

[x] Lean In; "The State of Black Women in Corporate America"; 2020; https://leanin.org/research/state-of-black-women-in-corporate-america/introduction.

[xi] Kamaron McNair, "56% of Americans say they're not on track to comfortably retire—how to catch up," make it, September 8, 2023, https://www.cnbc.com/2023/09/08/56percent-of-americans-say-theyre-not-

on-track-to-comfortably-retire.html#:~:text=Regardless%20of%20how%20they%20define,re%20emotionally%20or%20physically%20ready.

[xii] http://www.statisticbrain.com/new-years-resolution-statistics/

[xiii] Shahid, Kiran, "11 Surprising Goal Setting Statistics To Crush 2024," bramework, January 11, 2023, https://www.bramework.com/goal-setting-statistics/#:~:text=Research%20suggests%20that%2092%20percent,%2C%20specific%2C%20and%20realistic%20goals.

[xiv] Harter, Jim, "U.S. Employee Engagement Needs a Rebound in 2023," *Gallup*, January 25, 2023, https://www.gallup.com/workplace/468233/employee-engagement-needs-rebound-2023.aspx.

[xv] Montañez, Rachel, "61% Have A Transactional Work Relationship — Here's How To Change That," *Forbes*, December 19, 2022, https://www.forbes.com/sites/rachelmontanez/2022/12/19/61-have-a-transactional-work-relationship---heres-how-to-change-that/?sh=7dcc802141ed.

[xvi] Salomonsen, Summer, "Drop the hierarchy: Why people skills are more important than ever," Cornerstone (blog), https://www.cornerstoneondemand.com/resources/article/drop-hierarchy-why-people-skills-more-important/.

[xvii] Kolmar, Chris, "Average Number of Jobs in a Lifetime [2023]: How Many Jobs Does The Average Person Have," Zippia, January 11, 2023, https://www.zippia.com/advice/average-number-jobs-in-lifetime/.

[xviii] Vozza, Stephanie, "When bringing your 'whole self' to work could be a bad idea," Fast Company, January 25, 2023, https://www.fastcompany.com/90838250/bringing-your-whole-self-work-bad-idea.

[xix] Hartman, Mitchell, "How women raised the median family income," Marketplace, April 11, 2017, https://www.marketplace.org/2017/04/11/ive-always-wondered-family-income-women-and-work/.

[xx] Mitchelson, Ronald and James S. Fisher, "Long Distance Commuting and Income Change in the Towns of Upstate New York," *JSTOR*, 63, January 1987, https://www.jstor.org/stable/143850?origin=crossref.

[xxi] Pew Research Center, "1. Changes in the American workplace," October 6, 2016, https://www.pewresearch.org/social-trends/2016/10/06/1-changes-in-the-american-workplace/.

[xxii] Kochhar, Rakesh and Stella Sechopoulos, "How the American middle class has changed in the past five decades," Pew Research Center, April 20, 2022, https://www.pewresearch.org/short-read/2022/04/20/how-the-american-middle-class-has-changed-in-the-past-five-decades/.

[xxiii] Productivity paradox, *Wikipedia*, https://en.wikipedia.org/wiki/Productivity_paradox#:~:text=The%20productivity%20paradox%2C%20also%20referred,productivity%20growth%20in%20the%20United.
Bergeaud, Antonin, Gilbert Cette, and Remy Lecat, "Long-Term Growth and Productivity Trends: Secular Stagnation or Temporary Slowdown?" *Cairn*, 2018, https://www.cairn.info/revue-de-l-ofce-2018-3-page-37.htm.

[xxiv] Hartman, Mitchell, "How women raised the median family income," Marketplace, April 11, 2017, https://www.marketplace.org/2017/04/11/ive-always-wondered-family-income-women-and-work/.

[xxv] United States Census Bureau, "Census Bureau Estimates Show Average One-Way Travel Time to Work Rises to All-Time High," March 18, 2021, https://www.census.gov/newsroom/press-releases/2021/one-way-travel-time-to-work-rises.html.

[xxvi] Cantrell, Sue, Michael Griffiths, Robin Jones, and Julie Hllpakka, "The skills-based organization: A new operating model for work and the workforce," Deloitte Insights (blog), September 8, 2022, https://www2.deloitte.com/us/en/insights/topics/talent/organizational-skill-based-hiring.html.

[xxvii] Kolmar, Chris, "Average Number of Jobs in a Lifetime [2023]: How Many Jobs Does The Average Person Have," Zippia, January 11, 2023, https://www.zippia.com/advice/average-number-jobs-in-lifetime/.

[xxviii] Nguyen, Janet, "Money and millennials: The cost of living in 2022 vs. 1972," Marketplace (blog), August 17, 2022, https://www.marketplace.org/2022/08/17/money-and-millennials-the-cost-of-living-in-2022-vs-1972/.

[xxix] Mok, Aaron, "Hybrid workers spend an average of $51 a day when they go into the office," *Business Insider*, October 12, 2023,

https://www.businessinsider.com/return-to-office-costs-employees-hybrid-work-commuting-lunch-parking-2023-10.

[xxx] Symmank, Rebecca, "9 Corporate Real Estate Metrics You Should Be Tracking," Realcomm, June 17, 2021, https://www.realcomm.com/news/1035/2/9-corporate-real-estate-metrics-you-should-be-tracking.

[xxxi] Ducharme, Jamie, "Why Work Friends Are Crucial for Your Health," *Time*, April 26, 2023, https://time.com/6274502/work-friends-health-benefits/.

[xxxii] Markman, Art, "Why You May Actually Want to Go Back to the Office," *Harvard Business Review*, July 1, 2021, https://hbr.org/2021/07/why-you-may-actually-want-to-go-back-to-the-office.

[xxxiii] Cantrell, Sue, Michael Griffiths, Robin Jones, and Julie Hllpakka, "The skills-based organization: A new operating model for work and the workforce," Deloitte Insights (blog), September 8, 2022, https://www2.deloitte.com/us/en/insights/topics/talent/organizational-skill-based-hiring.html.

[xxxiv] Ito, Aki, "The end of workplace loyalty," *Business Insider*, January 22, 2024, https://www.businessinsider.com/loyalty-employee-employer-job-security-broken-work-companies-bosses-2024-1.

[xxxv] Ellingrud, Kweilin, Saurabh Sanghvi, Gurneet Sing Dandona, Anu Madgavkar, Michael Chui, Olivia White, and Paige Hasebe, "Generative AI and the future of work in America," McKinsey Global Institute, July 26, 2023, https://www.mckinsey.com/mgi/our-research/generative-ai-and-the-future-of-work-in-america.

[xxxvi] *Ibid*.

[xxxvii] Mercer, "Workforce 2.0," https://www.mercer.com/assets/global/en/shared-assets/local/attachments/pdf-2024-global-talent-trends-report-en.pdf.

[xxxviii] Accenture, "The future of work is bright because of apprenticeships," https://www.accenture.com/us-en/about/company/apprenticeships.

[xxxix] Mercer, "Workforce 2.0 Unlocking human potential in a machine-augmented world," https://www.mercer.com/assets/global/en/shared-assets/local/attachments/pdf-2024-global-talent-trends-report-en.pdf.

www.ingramcontent.com/pod-product-compliance
Lightning Source LLC
Chambersburg PA
CBHW071422090426
42737CB00011B/1542

* 9 7 9 8 9 9 0 6 9 1 9 1 9 *

[xl] Gallup, "State of the Global Workplace: 2023 Report," https://www.gallup.com/workplace/349484/state-of-the-global-workplace.aspx.

[xli] Atkins, Charles, Olivia White, Asutosh Padhi, Kweilin Ellingrud, Anu Madgavkar, and Michael Neary, "Rekindling US productivity for a new era," McKinsey Global Institute, February 16, 2023, https://www.mckinsey.com/mgi/our-research/rekindling-us-productivity-for-a-new-era#introduction.

[xlii] Schwartz, Tony and Catherine McCarthy, "Manage Your Energy, Not Your Time," *Harvard Business Review*, October 2007, https://hbr.org/2007/10/manage-your-energy-not-your-time.